Aaron Watson, Lillias Wassermann

The Marquis of Carabas

A Story of Today

Aaron Watson, Lillias Wassermann

The Marquis of Carabas
A Story of Today

ISBN/EAN: 9783744760294

Printed in Europe, USA, Canada, Australia, Japan

Cover: Foto ©Thomas Meinert / pixelio.de

More available books at **www.hansebooks.com**

THE
MARQUIS OF CARABAS

A Story of To-day

BY

AARON WATSON

AND

LILLIAS WASSERMANN

IN THREE VOLUMES
VOL. I.

London
CHATTO & WINDUS, PICCADILLY
1892

CONTENTS OF VOL. I.

CHAPTER	PAGE
I. THE OLD MARQUIS RECEIVES A SHOCK	1
II. THE EFFECT OF A PICTURE	10
III. WHAT HAPPENED IN CHURCH	29
IV. THE NEW MARQUIS TAKES HIS SEAT	47
V. RELICS OF A DEAD MAN	67
VI. A COMMONPLACE LOVE-STORY	86
VII. A POET 'UP TO DATE'	104
VIII. IN A LAND OF DREAMS	125
IX. AN ADVENTURE IN THE PARK	143
X. JACOB DEAN SUSPECTS A MYSTERY	164
XI. A FAMILY HIGHLY CONNECTED	181
XII. BESSIE PUTS ON MOURNING	198

CHAPTER	PAGE
XIII. SURPRISING FAILURES OF MEMORY	216
XIV. A DUKE'S DAUGHTERS	236
XV. LORD CRANBERY MAKES AN ACQUAINTANCE	257

THE MARQUIS OF CARABAS

CHAPTER I.

THE OLD MARQUIS RECEIVES A SHOCK.

Solitary, in the great breakfast-room of Bexley House, his head thrown back on the high cushions of his chair, his eyes staring vacantly at the oak panelling of the walls, his hands limply clasped on his shrivelled knees, sat the Most Honourable the Marquis of Carabas, Knight of the Garter, Hereditary Grand Naperer of the Royal Household, Lord-Lieutenant of his county, and owner of splendid estates in each of the countries of the British Isles.

No pedigree more ancient or more sound

than that of the Marquis of Carabas was to be found in the pages of Sir Bernard Burke. He was respected for his character and envied for his wealth; he was constantly referred to as one of the best types of the old nobility, and quoted on public platforms as a living argument in favour of the House of Lords. Only a few days ago, when he had spoken on some question of foreign policy then exciting the public mind, one of the newspapers of his party had observed: 'In public and in private life the Marquis of Carabas is equally calculated to command respect and to conciliate affection. High-minded, open, dignified, generous, he clothes the sentiments of a patriot in the language of a gentleman. If his abilities are not so conspicuous as those of one or two other peers we could name, his understanding is sound, his motives are above suspicion, and he combines a real love of his country with pride in its institutions and its greatness. If we were asked to indicate one of the most perfect models of an aristocratic patriot, we should point to the Marquis of Carabas.'

But in spite of his rank, his wealth, his distinction, his long pedigree, and his public reputation, the Marquis of Carabas was, in that moment in which we first beheld him, no more than a poor, lonely, broken-hearted old man, with his pride humbled, his hopes destroyed, his great name ineffaceably soiled, with no affectionate heart to rest himself upon, with none to attend to him save hirelings, and unknowing of any who really cared, except in respect of some selfish interest, whether he lived or died. The pictured semblances of his ancestors, staring at him from the walls, were as near to and as much in touch with him as he was in touch with all the living and breathing world.

The Marquis of Carabas always wore a stiff and rigid expression, partly the consequence of reserve, and partly of an ingrained consciousness of rank and importance. Generally, also, he was alone, as he was now; for Bexley House had lost the habit of entertainment. The Marchioness of Carabas had been laid in the family vault for twenty years or more. There were no daughters of the distinguished house, and the only son visited his father but rarely, and was not welcome when he came.

This special morning, however, there was something striking and peculiar, and even awful, in the Marquis's loneliness. One who had then entered this room must have been drawn to him by the pathos and the pain of his face, even if he had been also repelled by the pride, haughtiness, and amazement of its semi-conscious stare. Yet such a one would, it is probable, have failed to arouse the least attention on the part of that lonely figure.

There are some men whose minds are wrecked and shattered by a single blow. They become inert, helpless, imperceptive, almost incapable of movement either of body or of brain. Theirs is that awful

'Death in Life' on whose face the Ancient Mariner gazed appalled. But the Marquis of Carabas had survived many a stroke of fate, which had bent neither his shoulders nor his will — which, indeed, had merely made him more dignified, more reserved, and more severe. Now, however, the greatest blow of all had fallen. In this dismaying moment the mind had no more energy to reassert itself. It was huddled up, as it were, tossed into billows, and frozen by the power of astonishment.

The white, keen, proud, and delicate face was drawn and rigid; the gray shadow of approaching death seemed to have settled upon it; the curving lines on either side of the nostrils had grown long and deep, like the seams of old wounds. The Marquis stared vacantly before him, without seeing, without power of movement, without capacity for thought. Yet an experienced eye would have discerned at once that it was not paralysis which had produced these singular appearances, this mental ineptitude; but a great horror and bewilderment, such as must have fallen on that French lady who believed that God would not damn a person of her quality, had she, when it came to the trial, found herself shut out of Paradise.

If one had asked what was the meaning of this strange and terrible look on the face of the Marquis of Carabas, it would not have been necessary to search very assiduously for the determining cause. That morning's *Times* had fallen from his nerveless fingers. It lay so folded on the floor that a single headline stood out plainly visible, with a smaller headline beneath. That there should be two headlines to any item of news in the *Times* is in itself an indication of the unusual importance of the intelligence which is thus set forth, and in this instance the lines were these:

GREAT TURF SCANDAL.

LORD BEXLEY AND THE JOCKEY CLUB.

It was a bare enough statement which followed. The reporter said:

'An extraordinary meeting of the Jockey Club was held at Newmarket yesterday. The sitting was *in camera*, but we are informed on the best authority that the Hon. John Logwood was asked to take the chair, and that the special matter for consideration was the in-and-out running of certain horses from the Donisthorpe stables. Charles Selvidge, the well-known jockey, was in attendance, and an invitation to be present had been despatched to Lord Bexley, but was not responded to. At the close of the meeting we were informed by Mr. Logwood that Selvidge's license had been suspended for two years, and that the stewards had resolved to warn Lord Bexley off Newmarket Heath. This,' it was remarked in conclusion, 'is no doubt an extreme step, such as has not previously been taken in the case of a man of Lord Bexley's rank and position; but the curious running of this nobleman's horses has been for a long time past matter of public comment, and it may be assumed that in a case of so much importance the Stewards of the Jockey Club had before them all the evidence which could assist them in coming to a just conclusion.'

This, then, it was which, coming with unexpected force upon an already enfeebled frame, had shocked the Marquis of Carabas into a condition much more resembling death than life. Lord Bexley was the last of his race, the successor to his estates and titles, the heir to an unstained name; and Lord Bexley was—his son!

A younger man than the Marquis might have stormed and raged and threatened, and have broken the force of so terrible a blow by the energy of his wrath; but Lord Carabas was old and worn, and rather weary, and the event shocked and froze his being, so that he had neither words nor tears nor cries, but was conscious only of a half-numb feeling of some great calamity; of a sudden, confused, deadening fall; of grief that should have found some expression, but was stricken and dumb.

And over all there hovered a dim sense of amazement, as if the thing which had taken place were something quite beyond apprehension and belief.

CHAPTER II.

THE EFFECT OF A PICTURE.

THE Marquis of Carabas sat long in this stupor into which he had fallen. It was the custom of the house to leave him entirely undisturbed during these morning hours. The great house was swarming with servants, but its owner could not have seemed more alone if it had been a cabin in the middle of a moor. Gradually and slowly his perceptions returned to him. He drew a long breath, shivered, drew himself erect, and by-and-by looked down at the newspaper which had fallen from his nerveless hand. The sight seemed in some measure to revive his energy. He stooped down hastily, gathered up the crumpled sheets, folded them with quick, nervous fingers, and stood for an instant as if he would thrust into the fire what had brought him the news of his son's disgrace.

'M' lud, did your lordship ring?'

It was his man, Farnley, middle-aged, scrupulously dressed, with a deferential bend in his shoulders, and an unusual appearance of curiosity and interest in his face.

'I shall go to the library, Farnley. Bring up anything that you think I may need. Let me see; it is the day before Christmas, is it not? Leave the lights in readiness, and I shall not want you further to-day. No—I think—not to-day.'

As he spoke he was conscious of compressing the newspaper in his hand, as if he would hide it from the eyes of his attendant. He felt guilty, somehow, before this man, and it seemed to him that his voice had almost a supplicating tone. The idea helped to shock him back into his former self.

'That will do, Farnley,' he said, with more sharpness of manner. 'I shall have no further orders to-day.'

As the valet retired, the Marquis turned to the fire once more, took the massive poker in one of his trembling hands, and prepared to thrust the obnoxious newspaper into the now expiring ashes. His attitude was that of some frightened criminal, who is about to destroy the evidences of his crime. But suddenly he drew himself erect, and the poker fell from his hands.

'Not now, and not here,' he said; 'the ashes will remain.'

This proud nobleman had actually become afraid of his own servants. They might find the charred remnants of paper in the grate, and guess how he had been employed. The newspaper was thrust hastily into the pocket of his dressing-gown, and then he leaned on the table for a moment, gave a weary look all around him, and finally went off with slow and measured steps to the library.

It was a long, large room, nobly furnished. The tall windows looked far away over the snowy landscape. There was already a flush of orange light on the horizon. The Marquis rose late—the days were the shortest of the year; and his period of stupor before the breakfast-room fire had lasted from the morning to the early afternoon. As the shadows crept nearer over the snow he paced from end to end of the spacious library, now with a quick and angry step, and now with the slow feebleness of age. Occasionally he would pause before some book, as if to read the lettering of its cover; but his eyes saw nothing at these times, and his mind was all confused tumult, with no impression clear and plain. At length he sank down into a vast easy-chair, placed his head in his hands, and thenceforward for awhile moved no more than a stone.

The diffused orange light in the western sky had died down into a single gleam of red, the room had become full of shadows, and the Marquis seemed asleep. Meantime there was much stir throughout all that enormous house, except in this portion, where he who owned it nursed his grief and shame. It was but a poor and futile expedient to hide the journal which contained the dreadful news. Evil intelligence has many and swift channels, and, from stable-boy to housekeeper, all who ate the Marquis's bread knew that Lord Bexley had been warned off Newmarket Heath, and knew also the full significance of that proceeding.

Farnley had watched his master upstairs, not without anxiety and misgiving. Then he betook himself to the housekeeper's room to talk matters over with Mrs. Dobson, who, notwithstanding a certain overdone stateliness, had a high regard for Mr. Farnley as a source of exclusive information.

'He's took it very bad, Mrs. Dobson,' the gentleman's gentleman observed, by way of introducing the great subject. 'I don't know as I ever see such a look on any human bein's face before, I give you my word for it. When he went along the 'all, tryin' to walk very stiff an' stately, his poor old legs was shakin' and tremblin' under him so that it was quite pitiful to see him. It was all I could do, I do declare, to keep from rushing after him to beg him to take a hold of my arm. But you know his ludship, Mrs. Dobson; and you know what he would have said had he seen me spyin' on him there.'

'It is a very sad business!' Mrs. Dobson remarked, with a long-drawn sigh—'a very sad business indeed!'

'You may well say so, Mrs. Dobson; and a business as will shorten the Marquis's life, too, I make bold to think. But I always predicted, as you know, that something very bad would come of Bexley's goin's on.'

'That has been too clear to all of us, Mr. Farnley; but could you have supposed that it would be so bad as this?'

'Why, you see, ma'am, you may expect anything from some men. When a man as has come to years of discretion shows a disinclination to enter the holy bonds of matrimony, and shows it all the more the longer he lives, as Bexley has done, Mrs. Dobson, what but the very worst is to be expected of him, I should like to know?'

Here Mr. Farnley paused, partly with a view of giving Mrs. Dobson leisure in which to reflect on the probable soundness of his own matrimonial intentions, and partly with a view of being pressed to speak on matters concerning which he had, in fact, no certain information.

Mrs. Dobson tried to look unconscious and indifferent, but feminine curiosity soon got the better of genteel reserve.

'Certainly, if anyone is acquainted with family matters, it is you, Mr. Farnley,' she said. 'Now, I have heard—everyone must have heard: for you know how these rumours are blown about, Mr. Farnley?—I have heard whispers of some entanglement, some scandal, you know——'

'Entanglement there may have been—entanglement there *was*, Mrs. Dobson: for, between you and me, I have seen one or two of Bexley's letters; but scandal there never has been about that matter, though about so many others. And for why? Because Bexley is very 'cute, you see; and if he has got himself entangled, as I do know that he has, it is noways in his own class of society, but most likely among the lower horders — for Bexley is low, Mrs. Dobson, Bexley is low.'

'And what do you know, then, about this entanglement, Mr. Farnley?' the housekeeper inquired.

'What I know is less than what I suspect, ma'am; but what I am sure of is as them letters come from a woman, and a woman as wasn't well eddicated—and a woman as wasn't well treated either, Mrs. Dobson. He is fastened somehow, I do assure you; but how he is fastened I cannot tell. Why has he declined to *rahnger* himself, as the French have it? A man at his age, too, with the duty of providing an heir to a family like this, and such a title as that of the Marquis of Carabas! Why, I should like to know, has he declined to *rahnger* himself?'

'That is what we should all like to know, Mr. Farnley,' the housekeeper ventured to observe.

But Mr. Farnley dimly felt that if he was to keep up his credit for knowing more than anyone else about the family affairs it would be necessary to balance the deficiency of his information by the profusion of his talk, and so he went on as if she had not spoken. He had a certain pride in his eloquence, and in the accuracy of his pronunciation of a few familiar but effective words of the French tongue.

'So long as Bexley kept gentlemanly in his vices one couldn't find much fault with him, eh, ma'am? Not as I means to be an advicate of immorality, Mrs. Dobson. I see what you would say, ma'am. No, I am not an advicate of immorality; but we have had our vices in this family before, as you know. Harrystocratic vices they were, such as are proper to the *hoo-tong;* but Bexley has the vices of the *can-ile*, ma'am, the vices of the *can-ile*. Now, if he had *rahngered* himself when he was young, how different everything might have been!' And with a sigh Mr. Farnley abandoned his mind to the contemplation of the vices that become the heirs to great titles and the bluest English blood.

Neither the housekeeper nor Mr. Farnley interfered with the preparations for festivity which were going forward in the servants' hall. They contented themselves with a quiet tea together, in the course of which Mr. Farnley still further accentuated his opinions on the dangerous tendencies of those persons who exhibit a disinclination to matrimony, but without eliciting that response which would have encouraged him to more directness of speech.

'I wonder what his ludship is doing of,' he said at length. 'I've got my horders, Mrs. Dobson, or I tell you that I wouldn't leave him alone for anything, except it was this nice chat as I have had with you.'

'All the same, I would venture before long to go and see what his lordship is about, Mr. Farnley.'

'Ay, and so I will, ma'am; but I am not the man, Mrs. Dobson, to leave *you* all alone on Christmas Eve without so much as drinking your 'ealth '—a speech which Mrs. Dobson very properly regarded as an invitation to produce a little of that comforting liquid, skilfully compounded of best Scotch whisky, lemons, and hot water, sweetened to a nicety, which Mr. Farnley made a point of tasting whenever he visited the housekeeper's room.

Meantime the Marquis had roused himself from his stupor. The darkness was all around him now, and, as he recalled his scattered senses, he groped about for the means of procuring a light. There seemed to be a fixed yet halting purpose in his mind. With a richly-chased candlestick in his hand, and with a vague desire to escape observation in a house that he felt, with a painful consciousness, to be full of eyes, he crept, a shrivelled and shivering atom of humanity, with scarcely a trace of his usual solemn dignity left, by stairways and corridors, until he came to the room in which hung the chief family portraits. The light which he bore glinted as he went on marble pillars, on suits of armour that had been dinted in bygone wars, on portraits of statesmen and kings.

Bexley House was celebrated among English ancestral homes as the splendid residence of a distinguished race. To-night the Marquis felt like a timid stranger in his own halls. For the first time the place seemed vast, and there appeared to be a reproach in every dim suggestion of grandeur which the light revealed.

It was a relief to find himself at length enclosed in the one room he had been seeking. He leaned on the back of a big armchair for a moment, for he felt weak, and was unwontedly troubled with a catching of the breath.

The quaint presentment of an old warrior looked down upon him. This picture was believed to be the portrait of an ancestor slain at Crecy. The Marquis held up the light and looked at the grizzled face, crowned with an upright shock of hair. Then, one by one, he inspected the faces of those who had borne his name. They were a handsome race, but, with all their beauty, they had a look of sturdy honesty and courage in their features. Their faults, at any rate, had been of a manly type. Not especially famous for their virtues, they had left no very evil names behind them. Such vices as they had were not, as Mr. Farnley said, beneath their rank. They had all done their part in the world, too. Some had lived nobly; more had died heroically. This one had fallen at Bannockburn, and that at Naseby fight, and the other at Waterloo. Not a coward or a cheat had there been amongst them all.

'It was left for me to bring into the world one who should dishonour that noble line,' the Marquis groaned, with sudden bitterness.

The numbing effects of his first shock were being displaced by gnawing pangs of agony, and he staggered under these as from the blows of some physical assailant. He was ashamed of the violence of the emotion that possessed him. There was something almost plebeian, he thought, in the way that it was permitted to shake him to the centre of his being. He was unaccustomed to the tyranny of great passions. There had only been one period of exaltation in his life, and now it seemed like a dream of some previous existence. A picture in front of which he had come brought it now before him with such force that he reeled, and would have fallen, but that, with an instinctive movement, he rested his hand on some object that stood near.

The picture represented a gentle-looking woman, young and beautiful, whose right hand rested lovingly on the sunny curls of a boy who might be six years old.

'Algitha and Greville,' he said. 'How beautiful they both seem!'

He forgot for the time being that this lovely boy was the son whom he had hardly kept from cursing. The proud, reserved, undemonstrative old man went back in memory to the one sweet, untroubled, quite idyllic period of his life. His wife had not been a woman of strong character, or of a pride and dignity corresponding to his own; but he had loved her. And the boy was a most beautiful boy—of that there could be no manner of doubt; and the Marquis had loved him, too.

'Ah, God in heaven!' he exclaimed, as the pain of his new wound again made itself felt; 'why did he not die when he looked like that?'

He could gaze upon the picture of his wife and child no longer. The power of seeing seemed to be leaving his eyes. He reeled and staggered as he turned towards the door of the room. Just then Farnley entered, and caught him by the arm.

The contact recalled him to himself, but he was unaware of the extent of the feebleness he had displayed. In a moment, and only half consciously, he was again acting a part.

'Is that you, Farnley?' he said. 'You came at the proper instant. I must have stumbled against one of the chairs, eh, Farnley?'

'Yes, m'lud.'

'My eyes are not what they used to be, Farnley.'

'No, m'lud.'

'You may see me to my room. It is Christmas Eve, I think. The waits will come to-night. Well, I shall not be awake to hear them. I am tired, Farnley—sorely tired—and must sleep.'

'He spoke like a hangel,' Mr. Farnley observed to the housekeeper somewhat later; 'nobody would have expected it of him—nobody in the world.'

But the Marquis did not sleep, for all his weariness. His son had murdered sleep. Those ancestral portraits haunted him through the long hours. He was half delirious from exhaustion and agony of mind. He tossed from side to side, every nerve of his body asserting itself in turn as a centre of pain.

He heard the boughs of the old yew-tree creaking beneath his window, and the persistent monotony of the sound seemed to become a further burden to his brain. But suddenly a noise of men's voices, rudely harmonized, and obviously engaged in singing, rose above the torturing monotone. Ah, the carol-singers! He had entirely forgotten them in this welter of vague and tormenting thoughts. He felt grateful, almost, for they did him the service of tearing his mind away from his grief, and he sat up erect and listened, as if he felt actual interest in these proceedings. Only one voice was singing now, and the words of the carol came clear and distinct on the midnight air :

> 'Lordings, in these realms of pleasure
>   Father Christmas yearly dwells,
> Deals out joy with liberal measure,
>   Gloomy sorrow soon dispels ;
> Numercus guests and viands dainty
>   Fill the hall and grace the board ;
> Mirth and beauty, peace and plenty,
>   Solid pleasures here afford.'

'Now for th' chorus, lads,' said a deep voice out in the snow ; 'happen his lordship's listenin';' and then, swelling out on the cold air, from half a dozen pairs of powerful lungs, the chorus rose :

> 'Far away, in Bethlehem's manger,
> He was born of whom we tell,
> Bringing to a world of evil
> Peace and joy unspeakable.'

There was a movement and a stamping of feet as the last note died away. The carol-singers were thinking of good things edible and quaffable, now awaiting them in the servants' hall. The Marquis's thoughts turned to his own ineffaceable grief.

Gladness unspeakable because of the birth of a Child eighteen hundred years ago!

Sorrow unspeakable because of the birth of a child no further back than forty years!

CHAPTER III.

WHAT HAPPENED IN CHURCH.

This serenading of the Marquis was a customary tribute to his rank. To the carol-singers themselves it was more important that they should gain the good-will of the servants' hall. Thitherward, then, did they now carry their voices and their instruments.

It was only a few years since an organ had been introduced into the parish church. Previous to that time the musical portion of the services had been dependent on certain accomplished villagers, who were accommodated with seats in a loft behind the pulpit, where they interfered seriously with the solemnity of the proceedings by frequently tuning up their instruments in a distracting way.

Their old position and dignity had been sacrificed to the new-fangled notions of those to whom an organ had become an indispensable adjunct of worship; but they were still 'the band' of the village, and it would have been a grave invasion of their privileges if any others had gone round carol-singing on Christmas Eve.

Lately, however, they had sustained a loss. Their performer on the violoncello had died, and for this night they had been obliged to ask a man who played in the little Primitive Methodist chapel to join them. They were glad enough of his help, but were to a man determined to express no such obligation, for, from their point of view, 'a Primitive' belonged to an order of beings distinctly inferior to their own.

'I hope, Abr'am Nettlefold,' said the leader of the band, as they were skirting the great house in order to arrive at the servants' quarters, 'as yoe didn't think as yoe was kaping time in that chorus?'

'Ay was I,' replied Abraham, who was a small, lively, shrill man, with what he called an 'independent stomach.' 'Better time than some o' yoe, I doubt.'

'Yoe Primitives are just as conceited as yoe are good for naught,' said the leader, with some asperity. 'As long as yoe mak' a row of some sort, yoe care nayther for time nor tune. Yoe dunner, for sure! For a bar or two yoe are as slow as if yoe were winding up watter from a well, and th' next bar yoe tak' as if yoe were emptying th' bucket into a ditch.'

'If that's what yoe think, Isaac Welford,' Abraham queried, 'why did yoe exe me to bring my 'cello here?'

'Because,' said Isaac, 'we had a notion as yoe would be better than nub'dy; but it sames as if that was a big mistake, Abr'am, that it does.'

'Happen yoe'd like me to goo back again,

an' leave yoe to dow without th' 'cello at all?'

'I dunno quite say as yoe should goo back, Abr'am,' said Isaac Welford; 'but yoe arena much use here, and that's th' fact. But I should be sorry to stand i' th' wee of yoe gettin' yore bite an' yore sup.'

'An' I shouldna goo back if yoe did exe me, ayther. I'm nobbut a little un, but I'm as hungry an' dry as th' biggest on you. Yoe'll see as my teeth can keep time if my 'cello doesn't, Isaac Welford.'

'If thy teeth are as sharp as thy tongue,' said another of the carol-singers, 'thate soon be th' leader o' this cump'ny. There's nub'dy as can doubt that.'

'Come neaw, lads, let's strike up,' said another of the singers, whose deep voice sounded like something rumbling underground. 'We're in th' front of th' kitchen windows, and it's here as we mun do our best; for it's here as there's grub and grog, and many a jolly maid as well.'

'Ay, lads, strike up th' same carol again, and let 'em know as how we are here,' said Welford. 'There'll be some ale posset, I doubtna, and I should be woefully sorry to think as how it was gettin' cowd.'

An hour later these same musicians were trudging their way over the snow to the village, in melancholy mood; for something had occurred to shorten the enjoyment they had anticipated, and, still more sad to think of, to curtail their supply of the best liquor they had tasted for a year past.

'Well, if that doesn't beat aw as ever I heerd on!' said Isaac Welford, with tragedy in his voice.

'It mun be many a year, Isaac, since yoe went whome sober from Bexley House on Christmas Day in the morning,' remarked Abraham Nettlefold, intending his words as an expression of friendly sympathy.

'Ay, that it is, lad. But did yoe ever see the likes of that? Drunk as a lord, ses yoe! Drunker than any lord as ever I clapped eyes on, and I've sane a few on 'em come to Bexley House before now.'

'And he wanted to kiss all the maids,' said the man with the rumbling voice; 'ay, and he wanted to dance with th' cook; and he wanted to put us all out of doors, saying as how he'd have no leathery-lunged carol-singers theer.'

'And out we are, Jabez Percival, and just as we was beginning to be at whome with our liquor; and on a mornin' like this, tew, when the wind comes keen enough to cut one into ribbins! Well, well; dang my rags if that doesn't beat aw as ever I heerd on!'

From which somewhat incoherent conversation it may perhaps be inferred that Lord Bexley had come home in a frame of mind intolerant of musicians and overkindly to housemaids.

The Marquis of Carabas had just fallen into an uneasy slumber, when he was aroused by the noise of wheels and of a hasty and careless entry. He needed only a moment in which to guess what this must portend. Whilst he was yet reeling from the stroke, the shameless son who had at once disgraced him and an honourable line had come home to brave that outrageous conduct out.

A paroxysm of rage seized upon him. He was now almost too weak to move, or he felt that he must at once have faced the insensible, bullying, audacious wretch who was the cause of his great misery.

What must he have felt, then, had he known that this irreclaimable son had at once made his way to the servants' hall, reeled in among the keepers of Christmas Eve, insisted on sharing in their festivity, and had finally fallen down helpless in the middle of a country dance!

When the cold, gray sunshine of Christmas morning peered into the entrance-hall of Bexley House, it disclosed Lord Bexley prone on a couch, the armoured semblances of certain of his ancestors appearing to watch over him.

He had declined to go to bed on any conditions. There was an empty decanter beside him, and a detachment of soda-water bottles. Beside him also was Mason, his man, a person of shrewd intelligence and indifferent morals.

'My lord,' he was saying, 'you must really wake up, you really must! His lordship, your father, would not like to find you here, my lord.'

'Go to the—the devil, you canting old humbug!' Lord Bexley replied in halting speech. 'Let him see me as I am. He knows me well enough, Mason. Why should I attempt to deceive him? Eh! did plenty of that when I was a lad. Greville Adelbert Shelburne, Lord Bexley, sails under no false colours, Mason, my boy.'

'But, my lord, the Marquis is ill; not himself at all, they say,' Mason whispered confidentially. 'Saw the *Times* yesterday, my lord.'

Lord Bexley started up on his elbow, stared about him with a flushed face for a moment, and then brought his mighty fist down among the bottles and glasses that stood beside him.

'Damn the *Times !*' he exclaimed hoarsely, 'and all the confounded treacherous crew !' A torrent of furious, passionate, blasphemous language burst from him. He cursed alike those who had been his confederates in vicious practices and those who had punished him for them.

'Well, I have heard you talk before, my lord,' said Mason, 'but you are a-going it now, and no mistake !'.

The interruption was followed by a further flood of evil language, but suddenly the words died on Lord Bexley's lips, and a ghastly pallor shot over his face, as the pallid lightning sometimes flashes across a thunderstorm.

What, then, had occasioned the change?

This, merely. A door had opened a few yards from him, and in the open doorway appeared the figure of his father, perfectly and carefully apparelled, Prayer-book in hand, on the way to church.

Since the agonies of last night the Marquis had made up his mind as to his demeanour to his son and to the world. He would fall back upon his pride and upon the greatness of his name. The son should not be acknowledged by word, or deed, or thought; the world should see what a British peer could endure without flinching.

Here, in a most desperate form, the first trial to his resolution presented itself. The son lay there before him, an embodiment of evil passions and of evil living, surrounded by the tokens of a debauch, and fresh from the field of his infamy.

The Marquis staggered for a moment; he felt his limbs again grow feeble, but with an almost superhuman effort kept down the rising flood of his anger and shame, and conquered his physical weakness.

Slowly and with great stateliness of demeanour the old man crossed the hall as if he had perceived nothing, and, passing out of the door and down the snow-covered steps, took his way across the park, his feet sinking at each tread into the thin covering of crisp and glittering snow.

His son looked after him with astonished eyes. The sound of the Christmas bells smote upon his awakening consciousness. The 'music nearest heaven' was like a memory and a reproach to his dulled yet living conscience.

'Mason,' he said, 'I think I will go to bed now.'

'Yes, my lord;' and Mason offered his arm to the reeling man.

'I say, Mason, rather queer of the old boy, wasn't it? Wouldn't speak a word, either good or bad.'

'I should say it was very queer, my lord.'

'Doocid queer! I don't like it, Mason. Wish I had gone to bed when you asked me.'

'I wish you had, my lord.'

'I wouldn't have minded a row, you know, not a bit of it; should rather have liked a row, I fancy. But I don't like that confounded silence and that look as if he didn't know who I was. Didn't he seem pale, too, Mason?'

'He seemed very pale and very ill, my lord.'

'Ah! it has hit him hard, this has—it has hit him very hard. And, Mason, I'm a confounded scoundrel!'

The man discreetly made no response to this self-condemnation. For the first time he beheld his master in a fit of contrition, and though it may have been a holy, it was not a cheerful sight. Mason, therefore, after guiding Lord Bexley to his room, rapidly performed the necessary offices and slipped off to his own bed.

Meantime the Marquis, walking feebly, but with a certain resolute stateliness, reached the gate of Bexley churchyard. The villagers who had arrived to take part in the service of Christmas morning waited with doffed hats and bowed heads for his lordship to pass. There was an ingrained awe of nobility in their nature, for they had inherited reverence for the great house and its occupants along with their peculiarities of speech.

It appeared to these folk a thing in nowise strange or to be complained of that in the house of God, in the gray little church of their village, a gilded and painted railing, behind which the great people from Bexley House worshipped, should give emphasis to the inequalities of our earthly state. There was not a rebel in the village, even among the despised 'Primitives.' The Marquis, the Marquis's appropriation of almost one-half of the church to himself, the Marquis's grandeur and greatness, were all loyally accepted as a necessary and inevitable part of the order of nature.

On this Christmas morning the Marquis of Carabas entered his great railed-off enclosure alone. Whence he sat he might behold part of the little side-chapel where many of his ancestors slept in their marble tombs. Nearest of all was the recumbent effigy of a knight, his hands folded before him, a hound crouching at his feet.

This tomb fascinated him. He could not turn his eyes from it. The prayers, the hymns, passed over unheeded. He kept counting the bosses in the ornamental work of the long-familiar tomb.

It was an odd thing, but every time he counted them they seemed to differ in number. Eight, was it? No, only seven. Nine this time. How very singular and unaccountable! He must have known the number exactly, too, and from of old, yet —most astounding circumstance!—he could not bring it to his mind. He counted the bosses again and again.

> 'The parson droned from the pulpit,
> Like the murmur of many bees;'

but the Marquis of Carabas heard nothing of what he said. Those elusive bosses were troubling him greatly. They seemed as if they were receding into a misty distance, too. Could it be that he was becoming drowsy? He had never yet gone to sleep in church. It was the duty of so great a man to keep awake, as an example to his inferiors.

Now, however, a sensation of numbness was creeping over him. There could be no doubt of that. All his trouble seemed to be lifted, or to grow trivial and unimportant, all his sense of humiliation to pass away. He felt happy almost, but so drowsy, drowsy, drowsy. What could it mean?

The Marquis of Carabas sat stiff and upright, as he had sat while yet a man in his prime. Gazing still on the ever-receding effigy of his ancestor, it appeared to him as if he fell asleep and dreamed a dream.

A dream it was, indeed, and yet a dream that was grimly real.

His own hands seemed to be falling into the rigid pallor and cold stiffness of those of the recumbent knight; he felt as if he also were turning into stone. An enormous and ever-accumulating weight oppressed him. It bore him downwards, always downwards; and that seemed natural enough, for the figures on tombs—are they not all recumbent, and with eyes eternally closed? And in this strange dream of his he was aware that he was himself turning into a figure on a tomb—a figure of marble, senseless and cold.

Slowly, gently, without power of resistance on his part, and yet with as much quietude as though his motion were guided by his will, he slid down from the seat, on which his arms rested without clinging; and then he lay, still as that stone ancestor, on the floor of the church.

The Vicar had left the pulpit before this time, or he would certainly have noted the uncommon spectacle of the scrupulously decorous Marquis lying down upon the floor of his pew like one intoxicated.

From the organ-loft the voluntary went pealing on, and the church was all but emptied of its congregation.

The Marquis was usually among the first to leave, the people reverently waiting for him to pass, as if he had been the real object of their worship. As he did not come now, one of the two footmen who had followed him, without instructions, from Bexley House, crept timidly up to the great square pew, put aside a portion of the heavy crimson curtain, and peered within.

This man's immediate cry of astonishment brought the congregation crowding back. The village doctor was among the folk. Could there be at last an opportunity for him? He had only been called in hitherto to the servants of the great house. If the

Marquis were himself to become a patient his fortune was made.

The doctor gently but eagerly raised the hand of the prostrate man and felt his pulse. No movement there. He turned the face up towards the light, lifted the lids, and looked into the pupils of the eyes. No light beamed thence.

As the first notes of the voluntary pealed forth the soul of the Marquis of Carabas had passed away. No marble Crusader could more than rival now the stillness and the impassibility of what remained.

CHAPTER IV.

THE NEW MARQUIS TAKES HIS SEAT.

'By Jove!' exclaimed Lord Ronald Tunbridge, leaping to his feet and throwing down his newspaper on the floor of the Grafton Club, 'if that frightful scamp Bexley hasn't succeeded to the peerage!'

It was early in the day, and there were only three or four members present. They formed themselves into a group at once.

'You don't mean to say that Carabas is dead?' said Mr. Halliwell Romaine. 'I remember——'

Mr. Romaine was a distinguished Q.C., and an interminable story-teller. His reputation outside the law depended upon certain gossiping articles in the Quarterlies, made up of reminiscences, anecdotes, and old scandal. His interest in events was exactly proportioned to the opportunities they offered for tale-bearing. The death of the Marquis of Carabas was quite a windfall to a man so far gone in his anecdotage. But on this occasion Mr. Halliwell Romaine was not permitted to proceed.

'But Carabas?' said Lord Ravensbourne, who represented one of the departments in the House of Lords. 'When and how did he die?'

'Bless me, I didn't look at the particulars, I was so startled by the news!' observed Lord Ronald Tunbridge, snatching up his newspaper and hastily glancing over the account of the Marquis's death.

'Died in church yesterday morning, quite suddenly,' he added. 'Killed by a Christmas sermon, by Jove!'

'A fate that will overtake none of us, probably,' Lord Ravensbourne gravely remarked. 'But it is a sad event, everything considered; really, as sad as it can be. I suppose Bexley will vote all right?'

'I don't care how he is likely to vote,' said Lord Ronald Tunbridge. 'If I were in the House of Lords I should much prefer to see him on the opposite side to having him seated anywhere in my vicinity. He is a cad, and a vulgar cad, too! His succession to the title is nothing less than a public misfortune.'

'And it is in particular a misfortune to Mandeville Shelburne,' said Mr. Halliwell Romaine. 'I remember Shelburne's father —he was Lord Algernon Shelburne, you know—marrying Lady Ellinor Gybert. It wasn't much of a marriage; but she was a fine woman—a very fine woman indeed. Her father——'

But here Mr. Romaine was once more subject to interruption.

'For the present, I fancy, Shelburne would prefer to remain in the House of

Commons,' said Lord Ronald Tunbridge. 'He is a rising man, and he has talents and ambition.'

'He is one of your party, too. It would be a grievous loss to you if he went to the Lords.'

'*Was* of my party, you mean. I happen to know that he has been offered the Under-Secretaryship for the Colonies, and that he has accepted it.'

'Take one from two,' said Mr. Halliwell Romaine, revenging himself for the cutting short of his reminiscences, 'and how many are left?'

'Enough to form a Government, as you shall see,' said Lord Ronald, with a gesture half of petulance and half of burlesque. 'But from one point of view,' he added more seriously, 'it would have been immeasurably better if Shelburne were now to become the Marquis of Carabas.'

Very much to the same effect were the comments made in the newspapers, though they were not expressed in a manner similarly frank. All the eulogies of the late Marquis concluded with a reference to the succession, and with a scarcely concealed regret that a peer of such worth and character should be succeeded by one of whom it was possible to say so little that was good.

Some of the weekly journals, and more particularly those which professed Radical opinions, were more frank. *Rabagas' News*, notorious for its Republican proclivities, and believed to have an enormous circulation among the working class, openly rejoiced over the injury that must be inflicted on the peerage by the succession of Lord Bexley.

'He has just been warned off the turf,' it observed, 'and now he will go into the House of Lords to assist in making laws for a loyal people.'

To do the new Marquis justice, he deserved almost all the evil that was said of him. He was unquestionably, as *Rabagas' News* took the trouble of observing, 'a bad lot.'

His characteristics were such as were by no means to be accounted for on any theory of heredity. His qualities, such as they were, gave no signs of having come to him by descent. If his character had been determined by hereditary peculiarities he should have derived a certain stiffness of morals and a haughty pride of race and of bearing from the paternal side, and much gentleness and refinement from his mother and her kin. But he seemed to be without pride altogether. He was obstreperously defiant of conventionalities; his tastes were beyond doubt vulgar; he had scarcely mingled with his own class except on the turf, and he had been seen driving to the Derby in a coster's barrow.

A man of this nobleman's rank does not arrive at the great height of being warned off the turf at a single bound. He climbs up by gradual steps, as to any other eminence. Lord Bexley's life, so much of it as was known, had seemed to be a deliberately calculated outrage against his order.

And not all of it was known. He had a habit of disappearing for long intervals.

Sometimes he travelled. Travel was, apparently, his only intellectual passion. When he had been away for months together he might be heard of from India, or from the Cape, or from Japan. It was equally probable, however, that he would reappear in a London police-court. It was almost invariably a police-court in the East End or in the Borough that was favoured by such reappearances. He could not have replied, as another young man about town had done, when he was asked the direction to Worship Street, that he was unable to say, because he was usually taken to Marlborough Street himself. The statement would not have been true. He had been to Worship Street many times, and to Marlborough Street not at all. From which fact, coupled with his singular appearance on the road to Epsom, it was inferred that he had formed connections among the lower orders of which those of his own rank who knew most of him had no sort of knowledge.

There was a Cabinet Council on the day that followed the burial of the old Marquis of Carabas.

'It is very serious, the succession of that fellow Bexley to the peerage,' said the Prime Minister, Lord Sawbridgeworth, when the business had been concluded. 'I should have been prepared to sacrifice a great deal if such a lamentable event could have been prevented.'

'It will be a capital argument in favour of Rossmine's schemes for reforming the Upper Chamber,' observed the Secretary for War.

'That is just it. By just so much as Rossmine's case is strengthened our own will suffer.'

'He will never, I suppose, have the effrontery to come down to the House,' said the Duke of St. Ives, who was President of the Board of Trade and a much-respected member of the Government.

'I know nothing of the fellow personally,' Lord Sawbridgeworth remarked. 'But nothing that I have heard about him would dispose me to think that he will be kept away by any right feeling or natural shame.'

'The d——d blackleg!' exclaimed the Secretary for War.

This was probably the first occasion on which such language had been employed at a Cabinet Council; but though it created a momentary astonishment, it was generally felt that it did only feeble justice to the character of the new Marquis of Carabas.

'If that young man had broken his neck on some fortunate occasion,' Lord Sawbridgeworth remarked, 'we might now have been congratulating ourselves on the succession of a peer who unites fine abilities to an estimable character and just principles.'

'I think your lordship has judged excellently in calling young Shelburne to office,' said the Duke of St. Ives.

'I think so, too,' admitted the Prime Minister. 'I have associated high expectations with Mandeville Shelburne, and I have not the least doubt that they will be justified.'

If the words spoken in Downing Street could have reached a set of rather sumptuous chambers in No. 1, New Court, Temple, they would have gratified Mandeville Shelburne almost as much as if a recent family bereavement had made him Marquis of Carabas.

His windows looked out past the Temple library, across the slow, dreaming Thames, to the tall, misty line of buildings on the Surrey side; and in intervals of marching, in an absorbed way, about the floor of his room, he paused to gaze at this prospect, but really without seeing it.

That he would one day succeed to the marquisate and the estates was one of Mandeville Shelburne's fixed ideas. He was now the next heir, but he was in no hurry. His spurs were yet to win. For the present the House of Commons was the field of his ambition. There was nothing that he so much coveted as a great success in that distinguished assembly; and he was succeeding. At little more than thirty years of age he was an Under-Secretary of State. A career begun so auspiciously—and at a time when, he admitted to himself, there were exceptionally few men of promise on that side of the House to which he belonged—might lead to anything.

Oh yes; he could well afford to wait for the marquisate. On the death of his father he had not come into possession of great wealth, but he had nevertheless a sufficiency for all his present purposes. Considerations of money counted for little with him just now, and the enchantments of title and high position were greatly qualified by his intense eagerness for Parliamentary success.

Mandeville Shelburne had been trained to believe that the political career is the highest that a well-born Englishman can follow, and he had thoroughly absorbed the spirit of his training. He had practised oratory from his boyhood. At Oxford, for two years at least, he had been the best speaker in the Union, and he had even for awhile been chairman of that society. He had no really distinguished talents, it may be, but he had all those qualities which disguise the absence of great talents. Genius, he had convinced himself, is a capacity for taking pains. He had high authority for this explanation of the inexplicable, and it satisfied him altogether, fitting exactly into the constitution of his mind.

To say that he was insensible to the greatness of his prospects as next heir to the estates and title of the Marquis of Carabas would have been entirely to misunderstand him. He was fully and keenly alive to all the advantages of his situation, but he was more than willing that such honours should be delayed until they would crown instead of impeding his Parliamentary success.

Indeed, they might not come at all. Suppose the new Marquis should marry? There would be an end to everything in that direction. And marriage was by no means improbable in one who had not long passed his fortieth year. This, too, could be borne by a man who could win his own peerage, who might some day be the First Minister of the Crown.

Mandeville Shelburne looked from the bottom of the ladder to its very top. What troubled him more at the present time than the possibility of the succession dropping from him was the more immediate possibility that his cousin might disgrace him by taking his seat in the House of Lords. That would be very bad indeed. Why should not the new Marquis go abroad—at least, until the public memory of his escapades had begun to grow dim?

But it was precisely this matter of taking his seat that the Marquis of Carabas was just at that moment thinking of. There was to be a division on the Deceased Wife's Sister Bill—a hardy Parliamentary annual. It is defeated in the House of Lords every year, partly by the efforts of the Bishops, and partly by a sudden sense of duty in those peers who never by any chance attend to their duties on other occasions.

It would have made Lord Sawbridgeworth wild with rage if he had known that among the peers whipped up for the critical division was the notorious Marquis of Carabas. So, however, it fell out. The whip had, of course, been intended for the late Marquis, whose name, by some inadvertence, had not yet been removed from the list of the supporters of the Ministry. It suggested to the new Marquis a previously unanticipated line of conduct. Why should he not go down to the House? He had as much right to be there as any other member. He had been cut dead at his father's funeral by almost every man of his own order there present. They would pay all due respect to the old lord, but they would not recognise the existence of his successor. Well, they could not keep him out of his rights and out of the chamber in which they sat. There, as he said to himself, he had decidedly the whip-hand of them.

'Mason,' he said, on the morning of the day on which the Bill was to be thrown out, 'we are going to London.'

'When, my lord?'

'Now.'

And that very afternoon the Marquis of Carabas, whose town house was in no condition to receive him, was installed at Morley's Hotel.

It was not merely in a spirit of bravado that he had resolved to take the position to which he was entitled by his rank. The deplorable extravagances which he had committed, to apply to them their mildest description, were in no sense the consequence of intellectual weakness. His mind might even have been called powerful, and he had thought much on many things since his father's sudden death. The old life had seemed to roll away into the distance, and he would have been deeply glad and grateful if other men's recollections of it could as readily have perished. For himself, he felt that he would be able to forget soon enough. A new sense of power and responsibility had come upon him, and in going down to the House of Lords he had an odd feeling that he was for the first time doing something which was becoming to the rank to which he was born.

When he presented himself at the door

of that magnificent chamber he was stopped by the attendant.

'Only peers are allowed to pass through here,' the man said, barring the way.

'Do you think I should be such a d—d fool as to come down to this place if I were not a peer?' was the reply.

'Beg pardon, my lord,' said the man hastily; 'what name?'

'The Marquis of Carabas.'

The announcement produced profuse apologies, and the Marquis, almost unobserved, for Lord Sawbridgeworth was speaking, walked in and took a seat.

It was a crowded House, for the members had answered well to the Ministerial summons; but the Marquis of Carabas observed, with some chagrin, that the seats in close proximity to his own speedily emptied of their occupants. He saw quite clearly what this meant. He was to be left carefully to himself, or, as he chose to put it, boycotted.

The debate would have been called lively by persons accustomed to Parliamentary proceedings, but to him it was uninteresting, and therefore dull. Also he saw many disdainful glances directed towards him, and he did not feel as defiant or as indifferent to them as he tried to believe. He felt very uncomfortable, instead. Quite a strange set of thoughts and feelings was crowding upon him, and it struck him as a new revelation that possibly the noble lords occupying the benches behind and before him might have good reasons for preferring his room to his company. Some of them might be as bad as himself; some of them were certainly not much better, as he had reason to know; but none of them had been found out to just the same extent.

The atmosphere of the chamber grew oppressive, and he seized his hat and went along the Lobby to the central hall. There he encountered Lord Ronald Tunbridge, coming from the House of Commons.

Lord Ronald never cut anybody. Those whom he did not like he preferred to lash with his tongue, or pierce with the stiletto of his wit.

'Hallo, Carabas!' he said, 'who would have expected to see you here?'

'I don't think you will see me here again.'

'Don't like it, eh? Shouldn't have expected you would.'

The two walked down the steps, int Westminster Hall, across the yard, and so on into Whitehall, talking of indifferent things. Lord Ronald Tunbridge was proceeding to his club, but he could not, or rather would not, ask the Marquis of Carabas to go with him there. He summoned a cab.

'By the way, Carabas,' he asked, as he stood with his foot on the step, 'haven't you travelled a good deal?'

The question had no relation to anything previously said. It appeared to be a sudden thought.

'A good bit, I dare say,' was the reply.

'Well, you take my advice, and travel again. Take a long spell of it. Try Texas, my boy. G. T. T., you know;' and with this parting advice Lord Ronald drove away, leaving the Marquis of Carabas in a condition of tremendous wrath.

CHAPTER V.

RELICS OF A DEAD MAN.

IF the Marquis of Carabas had been in the habit of reading the journals of the day he might have found in them much which had a personal interest. More especially did 'the new journalism' concern itself with his affairs.

'Lord Sawbridgeworth,' said a paragraph in *Veracity*, ' has introduced into the House of Lords what I suppose must be regarded as a Black Sheep Bill. It seems intended to weed the House of its more disreputable members, a process which, if it were at all thorough, might go very near to the extinction of the hereditary principle in legislation. I cannot say that I wish well to the Bill. If we are to have a House of Lords, I prefer that we should preserve all its absurdities along with it. It may then, as the Duke of Wellington predicted, go bodily some day, in a storm. Everybody will guess, of course, at whom the new measure is especially aimed.'

'By the way,' said the paragraph which succeeded this, ' the new Marquis of Carabas is more than forty, and unmarried. Should he die without issue the estates and title will go to his cousin, Mr. Mandeville Shelburne, who has just been appointed Under-Secretary for the Colonies in Lord Sawbridgeworth's Government. Mr. Shelburne is a very reputable man indeed, and is not without a certain capacity for political life. He is, however, weak on the side of Tory Democracy, and believes that he can bring about an alliance between the working-class leaders and the Primrose League.'

Wherever the Marquis of Carabas was

mentioned, it was hinted with uncomfortable plainness that if he were only out of the way a much better man would come into possession of his title. But of all this the Marquis was himself both ignorant and careless. His reading of newspapers was strictly limited to the sporting prints. His mind was like a house with the blinds down. Of the Black Sheep Bill he knew nothing, or he might have expedited the passage of that measure by placing himself inconveniently in evidence among his brother peers. In a fight of that sort he would certainly—to use his own characteristic phraseology—have shown game.

His accession, and the unpleasant event by which it was preceded, had placed him face to face with an apparently insoluble problem. What was he to do with himself?

His new position had brought with it an altogether unaccustomed feeling of responsibility, but it was of a vague and bewildering sort. Then, too, he was cut off on one side from the indulgence of his favourite tastes, and on the other, as he perceived clearly enough, from association with his class. If a man of such a character, so situated, does not take a wise resolution, he becomes a greater blackguard than ever. The weight of his self-contempt crushes him down.

The resolution taken by the Marquis of Carabas was that he would leave the country.

He had been wildly angry when Lord Ronald Tunbridge rather maliciously suggested this course, but the more he thought of it the more sensible the suggestion seemed.

Lord Tuflington, the heir to an ancient earldom, had recently crossed Greenland with a party of explorers. He had gone away because he had got mixed up in a scandal with a lady at a minor theatre, and he had come back in the character of hero. He had even read a paper before a learned society, and was said to be engaged in writing a still fuller record of his experiences for publication as a book. Society had taken him up with enthusiasm, and the old scandal was so far forgotten or ignored that he was being constantly stalked by matchmaking mothers. Here, then, was an illustration of what time and distance and adventure might effect.

No sooner had he made this resolve than he proceeded to carry it out. The Marquis of Carabas, with marvellously few ceremonies of preparation, crossed the Atlantic, with an ill-defined intention of going somewhere 'out west.' Mason was heard, on the landing-stage at Liverpool, to call him ' my lord,' and the news that a British peer was on board the steamer then about to set out was at once cabled to New York.

This procured him the honour of an interview before his feet touched land, and though the interviewer contrived to draw nothing from him but strong language, he tracked his victim to a hotel, ascertained his name, was thereby put on the track of some very savoury particulars, and on the following morning published three columns of the spiciest 'copy' that he had supplied to his newspaper since he became connected with the press.

It thus happened that within a few hours of his landing all New York was made acquainted with the history of the Marquis of Carabas, as well as with certain apocryphal embellishments. It was especially set forth that he could swear like a lord.

When, a few hours later, the ingenious interviewer discovered that his lordship had left his hotel, and then that he had left New York, he at once attributed this result to the scathing vigour of his pen. As a matter of fact, the Marquis had no more read this account of himself than he had read those other accounts which had appeared in England. He was simply restless, and therefore he had moved on.

When inquiries were set on foot, it was found that he had visited several American cities, always with Mason in his company. At length, however, all traces of him were lost. He had made a heavy draft on his bankers whilst at Chicago, and then he had disappeared from sight.

The men who sailed with Columbus were grievously afraid that they might come to the edge of the world, and fall over. If the planet had been constructed as these mariners believed, and if the Marquis of Carabas had reached its utmost verge, and then fallen into the illimitable abyss, he could not have sunk more completely and mysteriously from human ken.

There was no member of the British peerage less likely to be missed than the Marquis of Carabas. But at length the continued absence of news began to be the subject of public comment, even in his case. It was thought—and in some quarters even hoped—that he would never return.

'I seem to have done you an unintentional good turn,' Lord Ronald Tunbridge observed to Mandeville Shelburne. 'I think you owe me one, don't you know.'

'In what respect?'

'For sending Bexley away. You are not aware, perhaps, but that was my brilliant achievement. Alone I did it, as the fellow says in the play. A little advice that I gave to him in Whitehall one night seems to have made you the Marquis of Carabas. It does, upon my soul!'

'I am sure I am much obliged to you; but my own detestation of my cousin was possibly not so strong as yours, and I have certainly never brought myself to desire his death.'

'What does it matter whether you desire his death or not? There's no doubt to my mind that the fellow's dead, and as I am only a cousin at about the fortieth remove, I don't mind saying that it's a jolly good job too.'

It would be placing Mandeville Shelburne on too high a pinnacle of moral elevation to suppose that he was insensible or indifferent to the advantage that his cousin's death must bring him. Four years had passed over since he became an Under-Secretary of State. They had been years of more than average success, but also of more than average disillusion. He had thought little of the peerage then; he almost desired it now.

'Why shouldn't Carabas come back?' he said, in reply to Lord Ronald's last remark. 'A four years' absence is not so very wonderful, after all, especially in a man of his character, with no one of his own order with whom he would especially care to communicate.'

'Wherever Carabas went he would want money; and he would want a pot of money, too. Now, his bankers have not heard of him for nearly four years past. That means that he is not again likely to be heard of. If he were alive, he would be having his fling somewhere.'

'The fact is,' Lord Ronald continued, 'I should regard his death as a merciful dispensation of Providence. It may seem brutal to say so, but I should. I want you in the House of Lords, Shelburne! That will suit my book exactly. There is just one too many of us in the House of Commons when you and I are seated on the same benches.'

There was nothing ill-natured in the remark, and Shelburne was amused at its frankness, for he knew exactly what it meant.

Under the light and airy manner of Lord Ronald Tunbridge there dwelt as ambitious a spirit as needs to accompany even the most fiery of souls. During the last four years he had risen to an astonishing eminence. He had not only arrived at a most important position in the Ministry, but had been the virtual leader of the House of Commons. Then he had taken a bold and adventurous step. A moment came in which he had to consider whether he could serve his future best by a great act of loyalty to his colleagues or by resignation; and he resigned.

His idea was that Lord Sawbridgeworth would ask him to come back; that he would be able to extort some evident but not very solid concession; and that he would thus by one stroke obtain greater power in the Ministry and additional influence with the people.

But the *coup* was, on one side at least, a failure and a disappointment. For once Lord Ronald had misconstrued his man. So far from asking him to come back, Lord Sawbridgeworth was furious. Of all qualities that a Minister could possess he valued loyalty the most. That any man should seek to improve his own position by placing his colleagues in a difficulty seemed to him to be monstrous. It was the one unpardonable sin. He had *made* Lord Ronald Tunbridge, he told himself. He had given him an office which scarcely anybody in the country thought him competent to fill; and this was his reward! on the first opportunity, the creature that he had warmed at his hearth turned round and stung him. Ask him to come back? Not if the Ministry must fall to-morrow; not if the whole country cried aloud for him; not if the consequence of obstinacy were to be his own permanent exclusion from power.

Lord Sawbridgeworth's views as to what he called 'this base desertion' were reflected in the chief organs of his party. Lord Ronald Tunbridge was alternately abused and lectured. He was reminded of his years, and of how becoming modesty is to youth. It all amused him very much. It was certainly disappointing not to be asked to again resume his place in the Government, but it was his future more than his present that he had staked on the throw, and, everything considered, he had won.

For the condition of affairs was this: that

whilst he scarcely dared to show himself among his old friends in Pall Mall he was unquestionably the most popular member of his party in the country at large. He had only to show himself on a platform anywhere, and the enthusiasm was unbounded.

But there was no demonstration against the Ministry at these gatherings. Lord Ronald was much too ingenious and calculating a politician to be led into the mistake of supposing that he could serve his interests by organizing opinion against Lord Sawbridgeworth. So far from desiring to create a split in the party, he was anxious to hold his party together. But, at the same time, he desired all the glory of independence, and all the importance that anxiety about his action must confer upon him. When critical debates were in progress it was invariably whispered about that he intended to make a strong speech against the Government; but just before the division there went round a confidential rumour that he did not propose to embarrass his party, either by speaking on the subject before the House or by going into the wrong lobby.

In his own phrase, a survival from his salad days, Lord Ronald was 'playing the waiting game.' Not, however, without a growing feeling of alarm. There was one rising politician whose popularity might some day come into competition with his own. This was Mandeville Shelburne. Lord Ronald had the knack of estimating himself pretty correctly, and he knew that Shelburne had some qualities more solid than his own. Besides, the former had stuck to the Ministry, and he might be the first to get to the top. There was a chance for one man to make a great success on their side of the House, but scarcely for two. He was therefore particularly desirous that Mandeville Shelburne should go to the House of Lords. All this Shelburne easily understood, being a man of more than ordinary discernment.

'But even if it should be the case that my cousin is dead,' he remarked, 'it does not seem clear how my own succession is to be brought about. How are we to obtain proofs of death?'

'That's the devil of it,' Lord Ronald admitted. 'Really, a fellow ought to die at home, where his friends would have the chance of soothing his last moments, and all that, you know.'

'No doubt; but for the present you must admit that your scheme of kicking me upstairs does not look very hopeful.' And with this remark the two friends parted.

The scheme, however, was ever so much more hopeful than it seemed, for on that very day a young American gentleman called on the British Minister at Washington and made a momentous communication.

'Can you tell me,' he asked, 'if they happen to have lost a peer of the realm out in your country?'

'Lost a peer of the realm? That is an

odd question. Will you kindly tell me just what you mean ?'

'Well, you see, I guess that I have found one—all that remains of him, that is to say; and it isn't much, that's a fact.'

'I must still ask you to make yourself more clear.'

'Well, you see, I've been out in Alaska. Pretty cold out there. I went in a sealing ship, and was landed for a spell. Thought I might not have the same chance again, so I let the ship go home without me, and came back over the Rockies.'

'A very interesting adventure, I have no doubt; but how does this bear on the loss of a British peer?'

'That's just what I am coming to. I came across some fellows who had had a fight with Indians. It was a case of scalping on one side or the other, so they took the Indian scalps. That was nearly four years ago. The Indians had been committing a murder, I should say. Had got a lot of things they didn't know what to do with, and the other fellows took 'em. Other fellows didn't know what to do with 'em, either, so I bought 'em, and brought 'em back with me.'

'And may I ask what these things are?'

'Impedimenta, I should call them. Seem to have belonged to somebody very well off—of the name of Carabas or Bexley, I should say.'

'Bexley—Carabas! Why, you do indeed bring important news! And do you think that Lord Carabas is dead?'

'I guess there's not much doubt of that. I've got his scalp in my portmanteau, and a good many other things of his. I've got a written statement from those fellows in Alaska, too. Gives the Indian story of the murder. Thought it might be important, so got them to put it down and witness it, and all the rest.'

'You seem to have acted with great discretion, Mr. ——'

'Marc. A. Tidd is my name.'

'Well, Mr. Tidd, you have acted with great discretion, as I have said. This is most important news. The Marquis of Carabas has been missing for these four years past. It will indeed be a Providential thing if you have really discovered how he died, and have brought the necessary proofs.'

'There's not much doubt about my doing that, I think.'

'Well, Mr. Tidd, the family, I am sure, will be willing to reimburse you for any outlay to which you may have been put, and, I do not doubt, to show their gratitude in any other manner you may think fit.'

'That's not what I want at all. They can have the things, and welcome. They can have them free, gratis, for nothing. I don't want either money or gratitude; but I thought I would bring the things along. You shall have them down here to-morrow, without fail;' and with this assurance Mr. Tidd bade the British Minister 'Good-day.'

When the 'things' came along on the morrow they left no doubt either of the fate of their owner or of the fact that this owner had been the Marquis of Carabas. They were transmitted to England at once, and within a short time of their arrival Mandeville Shelburne was called to the House of Lords under the ancestral title.

CHAPTER VI.

A COMMONPLACE LOVE-STORY.

At 10, Magnolia Street, Peppermint Hill, Clapham, dwelt Mrs. Elizabeth Shelburne, called by the neighbours Bessie Shelburne, and by her two brothers simply Bessie.

She was a small woman, with a fine, strapping son, and no husband that any of the neighbours had seen or heard of. An apple-cheeked, roundabout little body, this Bessie. She must have been rather pretty when she was young. She was still something under her fortieth year, but anxiety and hard work had told upon her, had robbed her of her bloom, and had streaked her fair tresses with gray.

Yet withal no lapse of time had been able to change the expression of wondering innocence which had been characteristic of her youth. Her round blue eyes and sweet, undecided mouth seemed rather to belong to the seraphically charming countenance of one of Raphael's cherubs than to a middle-aged, hard-working woman of Peppermint Hill. There was, too, occasionally an expression of bewilderment on her face, as if something had happened to her that she was too simple to comprehend, and a hint of expectation, as if the mystery were certain some day to be explained

How any woman could retain a mind so simple and so pure as looked out of Bessie's eyes in days like these, when wickedness flaunts itself, is proclaimed from the housetops, is published in all detail in every newspaper, was a puzzle to all Bessie's friends, and an especial source of wonder to her son.

But never did son and mother suit each other so well. The gay, buoyant self-confidence of the one exactly fitted itself to the timid reserve of the other. The relations of nature seemed almost to be reversed. Bertie Shelburne took a constant, fond delight in his mother's smallness, as contrasted with his own lithe, vigorous frame, and pretended that she was a person to be coddled and protected and made much of, after the manner in which a parent makes much of a favourite child.

What would she do, he asked, if she had not a son to look after her? Just wait till he was out of his time, and was earning journeyman's wages, and the world should see what a home they would have. Then it would no longer be necessary for her to take in work, either.

And to Bessie Shelburne protection came naturally enough. She had always been used to it. Her brother, Jacob Dean, was a year younger than herself; but he might have been twice her age, considering how he had ruled her from childhood. He would have saved her from what he considered to be the one great mistake of her life if she had only treated him with that confidence which, he contended, he had a right to expect.

'If you had done as I wanted you to do, Bessie!' was the prelude of many of his speeches to her; but on those occasions he somehow always had to change the subject. Ruled in almost every detail of her life by her strong masculine belongings, there was one point on which Mrs. Shelburne would listen to no criticism, no advice, no reproach. Jacob was invariably warned off the ground when he approached her affairs matrimonial.

There was an impression afloat in the Peppermint Hill neighbourhood that there had been something very wrong with her marriage, even if she had been married at all; but as for herself, she made no confidences on the subject. There was all the more conjecture because of her reticence. The gossips, indeed, deplored her ill-advised secrecy. They were sorry to be obliged to doubt whether she had ever really had a husband; but they had never seen her in mourning, and no husband had ever come to Peppermint Hill. And there was the boy, and—and—— But the head-shaking and the insinuation may very readily be left to the reader's imagination.

Whatever conjectures might be indulged in as to Bessie's past—and there was ample room for conjecture, seeing that the enigma already existed when she went to reside at Peppermint Hill—it was powerfully indicative of the character of the shy little woman, and of the restraining influence of her gentle spirit, that nobody ever ventured to hint a doubt to her of her own irreproachability.

The story that the neighbours would have been glad to know was simple enough in its main outlines. Bessie had married a man of whom she knew no more than that he had a handsome face and figure, that he professed at one time to worship the ground she trod on, and that he seemed to belong to some order of mankind that was quite outside the lines of her narrow experience. He had stipulated that the marriage should take place without the knowledge of her brother, Jacob Dean, otherwise the ceremony was all right and regular enough. Bessie had a copy of the marriage-lines among her treasures. It was a comfort to look at them now and then. An armful of railway scrip would not have been so precious as the now soiled sheet of blue paper which bore testimony to the fact that Adelbert Shelburne and Bessie Dean were man and wife.

It was almost twenty years ago now that Bessie had met her sweetheart for the first time. They had encountered each other at the Crystal Palace, whither Bessie had gone in the company of Jane Ann Sayers, and much against the will of her brother Jacob, who since the death of their parents had stood in the paternal relation, the elder brother,

Joshua, being rather in need of guidance than capable of extending any protection to others.

Jane Ann Sayers was a romantic girl. Her imagination had been fed on the *London Journal* and the *Weekly Budget*. Her daily expectation and hope was to become the heroine of some romance. Nothing in the way of adventure could have surprised her, for in stories that are to be 'continued in our next' the most astonishing things occur in every page. To Jane Ann, therefore, it seemed at once natural and delightful that, when they found themselves persecuted by unpleasant attentions, a young man of quite distinguished appearance should turn up in the nick of time, send their persecutor sprawling on the grass, and offer his protection for the rest of the evening.

Jane Ann decided that their timely rescuer must be a baronet at least. She confided as much in a whisper to Bessie. 'He's either a baron or a baronite, I'm sure,' she declared, when he had left them for a moment in order to obtain some refreshment. 'This is quite a roemance, Bessie—just as it happens in the stories. In one that I once told you about the baron is in a penny steamboat a-going down to Rosherville, and there he meets a young lady in the retail 'aberdashery line. What does it lead to, my dear? Why, a coronet—nothing less: all of sparkling jewels, such as you never see. Then there is a presentation at Court, and di'monds, and kissing of her Majesty's hand. It's too beautiful for anythink! Oh, Bessie, do look at the proud an' 'orty curl of his nostril!'

This last observation was made as the young man of the proud and haughty nostril returned with a waiter by his side, bearing the refreshments he had gone to procure.

Bessie did not much like the adventure. She could not help wondering what Jacob would think. Yet her imagination went a-woolgathering, too, especially as she noticed more and more that whilst their companion seemed amused by Jane Ann, laughing at her most serious observations, he was altogether deferential to herself. This, indeed, led to a quarrel between the girls before the night was over, Miss Sayers discovering that if there was to be any 'roemance' it was not for her, and declaring, much to Bessie's dismay, that she would go home at once, and alone.

It was a not unnatural consequence of this unexpected little tiff that Bessie should permit herself to be 'seen home' by her new and romantic acquaintance. In reality there was very little that was romantic about him. He was rather horsey in appearance. Persons of larger worldly experience than Bessie might have been unable to classify him quite accurately in other respects, but would have been pretty unanimous in surmising that he was some variety of blackleg.

Yet he behaved himself very well—like a perfect gentleman, Bessie thought—and he really was handsome, though his dress was eccentric, and there was a look of early dissipation on his face. Bessie attempted to be critical, but failed in the attempt. Before her companion parted from her that evening she was desperately in love.

There was many a meeting and parting after that. These were secret always. Bessie had no desire to tell Jacob; he would have been interfering, and would have wished to know too much. Joshua was a poet, and might be expected to sympathize with lovers, but he was also a helpless kind of person, and there could be no use in telling him. Yet a *confidante* was necessary, and who was there handy for this useful office but Jane Ann Sayers?

The two girls had made it up again, with many expressions of contrition on the part of Bessie, and many avowals that she never, never could feel the same again on the part of Miss Sayers.

It was, however, Jane Ann who officiated

as bridesmaid on the morning when, just after Jacob had gone to his work, Bessie Dean crept quietly out of the house, and, in a dull little church at Limehouse, was married by special license to the man to whom she had given her heart.

Jane Ann had been all the more ready for reconciliation because she had abandoned her belief in the exalted condition of Bessie's lover. He made no pretence to be of higher rank than Bessie's own, and the special license was the first indication that he possessed expensive tastes. Bessie, in her innocent way, had neglected to ask for any of those particulars which any prudent woman would have taken care to know. She had trusted everything to a man of whom she knew nothing at all; and, to do him justice, Shelburne had never attempted to take advantage of her innocence. What may have been in his mind who can pretend to say? What happened was this:

The husband, much to the simple little

wife's amazement, spent money freely after the marriage. They even went abroad. When they returned, Bessie found herself installed in a pretty little house at Walthamstow. Jacob called to see her now and then. But he would never sit down, and would, indeed, scarcely enter the door. Bessie had posted a penitent little letter to him on the day of her marriage, but Jacob remained ill at ease on the subject, and, to a certain extent, unforgiving. He thought there was something not quite right, for one thing. Somehow, he was never able to see the husband, his new brother-in-law, or to learn anything certain about him. He was almost brutal with his sister until she showed him the marriage-lines, and even then he was only relieved, not contented.

Jacob made a vow, therefore, never to sit down in his brother-in-law's house until asked by that brother-in-law himself to listen to an explanation of his circumstances.

From Bessie he could really learn nothing definite. She knew little, but would not tell all that she knew—that her husband remained away from home for long intervals, for example ; that he seemed to have no work to do ; that sometimes when he visited her he came on horseback ; that these visits were much less frequent than of old ; and that she was becoming grievously apprehensive lest some day she should find herself deserted.

On the birth of the little boy these fears vanished for awhile. Her husband visited her more frequently, and remained for longer periods. The child appeared to amuse him in an odd way. It seemed to be a joke to him, but a joke which puzzled and bothered him strangely. One day the mother heard him muttering to himself, as he sat looking at the little thing asleep in his cot. She caught disjointed sentences only. 'He's a pretty enough little chap, confound him ! . . . Poor little beggar ! . . . There will be trouble some day if this becomes known. . . . What a row, by Jove!'

The little woman could make nothing of all this, and did not dare to question him. There had never been any quarrelling or harsh words between her husband and herself, but she felt that there might be if she pressed him in order to learn what she so much longed to know. She loved and worshipped him still, but was afraid of him in some way that she could not define; and so she bore with mystery and misery and uncertainty, fearing that if she exhibited any impatience something much worse might come to her.

And in the end come it did. One day, when the boy was about two years old, Bessie's husband kissed her much as usual, left her, and never returned. The little woman suspected nothing till she went to the child's cot and found a roll of bank-notes under the coverlet, and then, with the rapid intuition of a devoted affection, it flashed upon her that she had seen her husband for the last time, and this was to pay her for his desertion.

What grief and agony then rent the timid little heart only Bessie herself knew. But she bore her trouble all alone. She did not send for her brother. It was not for three months or more that she confided to Jacob what she then felt to be too surely true.

'The d——d scoundrel!' he exclaimed; and then a little scream, followed by a sob, from Bessie, warned him that he could just then only make more misery by venting his natural indignation.

He took a resolution to find the man, if he was above ground, to hammer him well, as he phrased it, and to drag him home to his wife and child.

But Jacob had very little experience of the world. He followed up one clue after another, but without effect. A policeman of his acquaintance had seen such a man driving a cab. 'It was one of the new cabs,' he said. 'One of Weevill's,' he thought—'yes, one of Weevill's it was. Rather a swell for a cabman, that chap was, but a good hand, make no mistake!'

Jacob Dean went to Weevill's to inquire after the missing brother-in-law.

'A driver named Shelburne,' said Mr. Weevill. 'Never had no driver of that name; certainly not.'

A certain furtive look in his eyes made Jacob inclined to doubt his veracity, and when Mr. Weevill had turned his back he inquired of some of the men.

'No, there had been no Shelburne there, as they knowed on. Chaps changed their names sometimes, but none of their men had left for ever so long. But if he wanted to find a cabman named Shelburne let him go and ask at Scotland Yard. They were all booked up there, safe enough.'

Jacob had got this cabman idea settled firmly in his mind, for of the bank-notes his sister had told him nothing ; so to Scotland Yard he went.

'There are more than fifteen thousand cabmen in London,' he was told. 'Was there a Shelburne among them ? Lots of Shelburnes, probably. Shelburne wasn't such an uncommon name as all that, surely ?'

Oddly enough, however, when the index was explored, there was not a Shelburne in the list. 'Shouldn't have believed it,' the inspector said ; 'but there it was—not a single Shelburne in the whole lot.'

It never occurred to Jacob that the police might assist him in any other way. He went away greatly disappointed, very sorry for Bessie, and frightfully angry with her husband.

Then he took the worst resolution that was possible in such a case. He was on the point of getting married himself; Bessie and her child could not live with him ; but they would live together as nearly as could be. He took a couple of the little houses in

Magnolia Street, Peppermint Hill, much to the wonder of the agent, who had never before let two houses to one man, and Bessie went to live beside him, never dreaming that she was thus cutting herself off from her husband, if he should ever chance to return.

CHAPTER VII.

A POET 'UP TO DATE.'

Sixteen years had passed away since Bessie Shelburne's husband had deserted his wife and child, with never a word of good-bye. The little woman had made a brave fight in the interval. She had left untouched the roll of bank-notes that she had found in the baby's cot—had never revealed its existence, even.

At first it was pride and indignation that forbade her to make use of the money of the man who had deserted her; but as time rolled by the idea of the husband who had treated her so ill became surrounded by a mist of kindly memories, and then she secretly hoarded the notes as a fortune for her son when he came of age. With so much money as that, he might become a master instead of a journeyman, and all the Deans had been no more than journeymen for as long a time as the family history went back.

The notes would have been in danger many a time if Bessie had been a less unselfish woman, for the problem of living had occasionally presented itself in almost insoluble forms. Jacob regarded her as a weak and helpless creature, and such, indeed, she seemed; but this idea was rather gratifying than otherwise to Jacob, for it enabled him to realize the more keenly the contrasted strength of his own masterful nature. He had come to Bessie's assistance in more ways than one. Then, too, Joshua, the family poet, had been useful, and of late years he had come to live with her in the character of lodger, so that, with occasional jobs of dressmaking, she was now getting on very well.

Her greatest difficulty had been to repel the curiosity of her son as to his father's history. She had nothing to tell him, indeed, knowing so little herself; but this fact only made the situation more delicate.

One night the lad came home with a quite unfamiliar gloom on his face. When his uncle Joshua had gone to the little back room to write more of those poems that were always being 'returned with thanks,' he took his place by his mother's side, seized her small worn hand in his own large palm, and held it in silence whilst he gazed at the fire in a troubled, anxious way.

Bessie remained silent, full of 'ill-defined fears.'

'Mother,' he said at length, 'I want to ask you a question.'

She pressed his hand merely, and he went on: 'It was about something I heard. I wasn't listening, but I couldn't help hearing it. Mother, I hope it isn't true?'

Bessie waited, puzzled and sorrowful; but

her head sank lower, and her face coloured to the roots of her hair. The lad's heart drooped within him as he beheld what he took to be a confirmation of his fears. But with the thought of how hard the truth must be for himself to bear, there mingled the idea that it must be still harder for her to tell, now that he had come to guess it. He put his arm around her, as he had been wont to do on happier occasions.

'But if it is true, mother,' he said, 'it shall make no difference to us—no more difference than I can help, at least. I wish I hadn't known; but I couldn't help hearing when they said you had never been married——'

Bessie gave a little scream, leapt to her feet, and ran upstairs in breathless haste. She had been prepared for questions about the lad's father, but she had not expected this. A minute later she hurried down with the marriage-lines in her hand, threw the well-thumbed document on the table, and then fell down at her son's feet, crying as if her heart would break.

The lad endeavoured to lift and to soothe her before he had given even a glance at the paper, but 'No, no,' she sobbed; 'look at *that* first.'

He did look at it, and his first sensation was one of violent anger against those by whom his mother had been maligned. Then he was full of rage at himself for the wrong he had done in his thought to one who only valued her own life in so far as it could promote the happiness of his. He took her in his strong young arms, and fondled her with mute pity and contrition, till the cherubic little face that had so lately been full of horror-stricken grief beamed again with love and admiration and delight.

It was a long time before the lad could bring himself to speak, so great was his consternation at the cruel mistake he had made, and his joy at finding that it *was* a mistake, after all.

'I am so sorry, mother,' he began at length.

'And I am so glad,' she said, interrupting him; 'we shall know each other better now, Bertie, shan't we, my dear? Oh, ever so much better! You know all now; and you will never, never think bad things of your mother again, shall you, dear?'

'I don't know quite all, mother,' Bertie said; 'but you must tell it me. You know, I am nearly a man now.'

'And so you are,' said Bessie, proudly glancing over his handsome and muscular frame.

'Well, you will tell me all about it, won't you?' he went on, determined not to be driven from the subject this time.

Then Bessie had to confess how little she herself knew. But everything about her married life she told him, embellishing the account with glowing eulogies of his father, for which, in truth, the lad seemed to have little taste.

'And he left you like that?' he asked.

'Just like that, Bertie.'

'And you call him a good husband? Why, I call him a scoundrel. Just that, and——'

The little woman was again in tears. To hear her son thus describing the man she had loved was like a rending of the heart.

'Don't say that, Bertie; you will kill me if you say that.'

'Well, perhaps he was better than he appears, if you were so fond of him,' the lad reluctantly admitted. 'But did you never try to find him? Didn't you hunt for him everywhere?'

'Your uncle Jacob did, and he says he has been hunting ever since.'

'Then there will be two of us now, for I shall hunt for him, too. And I shall find him if he is alive—you can trust me for that.'

'And what shall you do then, Bertie?'

'Why, I shall say to him things that I cannot say to you; and I shall bring him here; and I shall make him beg your pardon on his knees. But there, mother, I must go out and think it over. I shan't be very long; but I must go on the common and walk off my excitement.'

When Bertie Shelburne returned, his mother was sitting up for him, full of trembling anxiety.

'A little woman like you should have been in bed long ago,' he said. 'I have been a long time—ever so much longer than I meant to be. There! go to bed now, like the good little woman you are. I mean to have a chat with Uncle Joshua.'

He kissed her fondly, and even joyously, for his walk had done him good. What he had heard early in the day had proved to be untrue, and the knowledge of its untruthfulness was so pleasant a sort of knowledge to have that it quite banished the dismal story of his father's desertion.

Uncle Joshua's room was scarcely an

ideal domicile for a poet. It looked out upon a back-yard, where a forest of clothes-props budded into branches of ropes, whose fluttering foliage resembled evergreens in the fact that it never seemed to be shed.

But, as Joshua said, the Muse is superior to her surroundings. She visited Bloomfield at a cobbler's stall, and John Clare when he sought to procure a warm bed by sleeping on a lime-kiln. Why shouldn't this same kindly Muse visit Magnolia Street, Peppermint Hill, Clapham? There was one verse of an American poet that Joshua was fond of quoting. It ran something after this fashion:

> 'A man should live in a garret, aloof,
>   And have few friends, and go poorly clad,
> With an old hat stopping the chink in the roof,
>   To keep the goddess constant and glad.'

'Ah, so he should,' Joshua would remark to himself, which, it will be admitted, was a comfortable doctrine for a half-destitute poet to hold.

The thin blind was down, and the back-yard was shut out, and a tallow-candle was burning, when Bertie Shelburne entered his uncle's room. There was nothing whatever that he desired to say, but he had just looked in for company. When he found 'the poet's eye in a fine frenzy rolling,' and the poet himself spluttering with a pen over a sheet of foolscap, he rummaged about amongst the books for a few minutes, then pulled a chair to the fire, and sat down to wait until his uncle Joshua should be more at liberty.

'Thank God that's done!' said the poet, at length, throwing down his pen. 'Hullo, Bertie, my lad, are you here? I never heard you come in; upon my word I didn't! You see what it is to have the divine afflatus upon you.'

'The divine afflatus seems to lead to the waste of a great deal of good paper,' Bertie observed. 'Look here, Uncle Josh, why not get some paper from the grocer? It would be ever so much cheaper than what you get now, and it would do just as well to come back through the post, wouldn't it? It needn't be a bit heavier, you know.'

'Do you think the editors of such magazines as the *Cornhill* and *Temple Bar* would look at poems written on tea-paper, Bertie, my lad?'

'Do they look at your poems now? Tell me that, Uncle Josh!'

'Oh, they must look at them, I suppose. It is only courtesy to look at them, you know.'

'But they come back, all the same.'

'That is because I am not what can be called a popular poet, Bertie. Just let me explain. It is a matter that I have thought over many a time. Every poet has to create the taste by which he is appreciated. Now, I have never had an opportunity of creating a taste for my works, my boy.'

'Because they never get into print, eh, uncle?'

'That's just it. Let me explain another branch of my theory. The poet must devote his whole life to the creation of poetry. Plain living and high thinking, as Wordsworth said.'

'Well, Uncle Josh, you've had plain living enough, haven't you?' Bertie inrupted.

'Plenty, my lad—plenty. Oh, abundance, I assure you! and I think I may say, without flattering myself, that I have done a good deal of high thinking, too.'

'Well, then, there are the two conditions of success, and no success after all?'

'Because, as I said, the poet must create the taste by which he is appreciated. Besides that, he must have means to live a life of ease and contemplation. Besides that, again, he must have means to put himself into print.'

'That seems to be the difficulty with you, at any rate, Uncle Josh.'

'Oh, I acknowledge it, my lad—I

acknowledge it with sorrow. For me the lack of means has resulted in a wasted life —not all wasted, though,' he added quickly, with a gleam of joy on his face ; ' they are all here, the poems are—in this box— flowers that are wasting their sweetness on some pieces of deal board.'

' That's a very poetical idea, Uncle Josh !'

' So it is—so it is ; but, though I say it myself, I think that most of my ideas are poetical.'

' It's a great pity that you can't turn them to account.'

' But steady, Bertie, my lad, steady ! What do you think I am doing now ?'

' I give it up.'

' Why, turning my ideas to account. Turning them into coin of the realm ! You know old Smith, the chemist ?'

' Yes.'

' Well, he's invented something, and patented it ; and he's going to advertise, and he's engaged me for his special poet.'

'The dickens he has!'

'That is just what he has done. It opens out bright vistas for the future, my lad. Just look at it in this light: I make money by working for old Smith; I save, of course; with my savings I publish a collection of my poems; then I leap at once into fame!'

'Without creating the taste that can appreciate you?'

'Oh, that must grow rapidly when once my poems are before the world.'

'And is this work of Smith's easy to do?'

'Easy? good gracious, no! Didn't you see how it was torturing me when you came in? You know a little about poetry yourself, Bertie. You have read a good deal, for your age—quite a wonderful lot for an engineer's apprentice. Well, what I ask you is this: just think what poetry is, and then tell me how you are to work in such a twister of a word as "aurora-vine"!'

'It does seem rather a clincher, I admit,' said Bertie.

'"To what base uses may we come at last": to be rhyming to "aurora-vine"; to be poet to a chemist; to put Pegasus in harness, as Longfellow said! It is cruel, it is infamous, it is too fearful a degradation of the Muse!'

'Why don't you drop it then?' Bertie bluntly inquired.

He looked at his uncle with a quizzical aspect. There seemed nothing ludicrous to him in the figure, for he was accustomed to it; but to a stranger Uncle Josh would have appeared a very odd creature indeed. His hair was long, of course, as much, perhaps, because hair-cutting costs money as because long hair is believed to be inseparable from the vision and the faculty divine. He had large eyes, rather wild-looking, but also with a sort of kindly shrewdness in them; his face was as long and thin as that of Don Quixote; he was tall, loose-jointed, stoop-shouldered, and his knees had a kind of giving-way appearance, as if they were much occupied in acts of adoration to his deity. During his fits of inspiration he increased the oddity of his appearance by the habiliments with which he clothed the outer man. His coat was of an indescribable colour. It might once have been olive-green, but had now assumed different shades in different places; it must also have once belonged to a man of shorter stature and wider build than his own, for it hung in bags from the shoulders, but was nevertheless short both as regarded the sleeves and the tails. His nether garments were of a large plaid pattern, such as every Frenchman believes that every Briton must needs wear. A pale-blue necktie with loose ends completed a costume that had at any rate the merit of originality.

However, it was not his uncle's costume, but his uncle's habits of mind, that Bertie Shelburne was inclined to quiz.

'Why don't you drop it?' he repeated.

'Because, as I hinted to you, Bertie, sad as it is, infamous as it is, I mean to turn it to account. "Aurora-vine" is certainly a difficult word, but it is not going to prove too much for me.'

'Have you been rhyming on it, then?'

'Oh yes; and with such results that I have been struck with an idea. If I can write poetical advertisements for Smith, why shouldn't I write them for other tradesmen, eh?'

'Why, not, indeed, and blow the Muse?'

'Bertie, my dear lad, I must ask you always to speak of the Muse with respect in this room. This is one of her residences, as we may say. I trust she will not desert me, though I do descend to write for Smith. But I will confide in you, Bertie. What do you think of this?'

He timidly produced a card from his pocket, on which Bertie read this announcement:

JOSHUA DEAN,
POET AND VERSE IMPROVISER,

Present Address:
    10, MAGNOLIA STREET,
           PEPPERMINT HILL.

Tradesmen and others in the Grocery, Drapery, and Boot and Shoe Trades, treated with for original verse composition for shop handbills, etc. Copyright and guarantees when desired.

No language used that would injure or shock the feelings of the young, or the most fastidious.

TERMS VERY MODERATE.

This ingenuous intimation was printed on cardboard of a flaring pink colour. The margins were ornamented with several more or less chaste and elegant designs, such as weeping willows, wedding bells, cherubs, and ornamental lamps, presumably for the purpose of burning midnight oil.

'I think that will fetch 'em,' remarked Uncle Josh.

'I should think it will,' said Bertie, bursting into a hearty roar.

'Why, what is the matter with it? Isn't it all right? I thought it was rather— rather nice, you know? It is the sort of thing that will impress people, if anything can.'

'So it will,' replied Bertie, half choking at every word. 'I am ready to lay money that it will knock 'em fast enough. Why, Uncle Josh, it's delicious! I wouldn't alter a word of it.'

'I don't think I will,' said Uncle Josh.

'Not a single word. I never saw anything better. That about not shocking the feelings of the young is quite a hit—as nearly perfect as anything can be. And "terms moderate"—why, you know, they can scarcely have come across a poet of moderate terms before.'

'I have heard of Tennyson getting ever so many guineas a line,' solemnly remarked Uncle Josh.

'Certainly; and you would take less than half that—or, say, less than a quarter.'

'I hope you are not chaffing me, Bertie. I didn't mean this to be comic.'

'Certainly not. I shouldn't think you did. But come now, Uncle Josh, let me see some of the rhymes you have done for Smith.'

'I will, since you like the card so much. Smith, you know, is the inventor of a new medicine. He has patented it. He insisted that I should try a sample. It is a beastly concoction of hops, gentian, and other abominations. That's what he calls "aurora-vine." If he would have permitted me to give a name to the stuff, I would have let you see what can be done when the Muse bends her soul to commerce.'

'But you have done pretty well, you say, even with "aurora-vine"?'

'Well, it does take a deal to floor me,' the poet proudly observed. 'Just listen to this:

> '"Whene'er the heart within is sad,
>   And life is duller than it's been,
> A potent charm can make one glad,
>   And that is Smith's 'Aurora-Vine.'"

Not bad, that, for a beginning, eh?' remarked Uncle Josh, running his fingers through his hair, and causing it to fly about as in a gale of wind. 'That is the ideal side of the new physic. Now for its other aspect, its practical one, you know. Listen :

> ' " It ill becomes a man of sense
> To pine from sadness or from spleen,
> When the small sum of thirteen-pence
> Will purchase Smith's 'Aurora-Vine.' " '

'Bravo, Uncle Josh!' shouted Bertie. 'You'll make a fortune. You are a genius.'

'Well,' said Uncle Josh, 'I'm almost beginning to think so.'

CHAPTER VIII.

IN A LAND OF DREAMS.

Out of the eccentricities of his uncle Joshua, of whom he was very fond—as who could fail to be?—Bertie Shelburne contrived to get a great amount of harmless fun, now that he was coming to a time of life when he felt his young manhood, and the stirrings of a bright, ardent, and cheerful mind within his breast. His uncle Jacob, as he sometimes observed to himself, was 'a horse of another colour.'

Jacob Dean was one of the men who make a kind of history which is seldom written, and which is still more seldom written with an understanding of its meanings and of its possible results. He was a leader of the working class, but of a new and, perhaps, on the whole, of a rather dangerous type. He belonged to no trade union, for he condemned such organizations with hardly less bitterness than he condemned the capitalists. In his opinion they existed mainly for the purpose of keeping ' the wage-slaves ' in subjection.

'We don't want the unions, with their smug secretaries,' he said. 'We are told that they have done a great deal for the working class. I am not going to deny but what they may have done so. All I say is that they have prevented a great deal more. Why, look here. You see this big stone pillar that stands behind me?' He was speaking to a crowd of miserable and hungry people on the Thames Embankment, and Cleopatra's Needle reared itself far above his head. 'They tell me it is ever so much more than two thousand years old. I dare say it is; but who made it, do you suppose? It was a big job of work, I can tell you. A block of granite like that wasn't easily quarried; and in such times it must have been a mighty hard thing to drag it to where it had to stand; and it must have been harder still to rear it upright in front of some Egyptian temple. And who do you think did all that? Just such fellows as you, with hungry bellies, and with misery in their hearts, and with the capitalist's slave-whip behind them. What has happened in two thousand years to make your lot better than theirs? The world has been getting on ever so fast, hasn't it? And how have you been getting on? You are as hungry as ever they were, aren't you? And you are just as miserable; and you suffer, as they didn't, from rain and cold. How much, then, have the trade unions done for you?

'You are pretty soundly discontented, aren't you?' Jacob went on to say, and there was a groaning response. 'I like to hear that. I want to make you more discontented than ever. I told you I wasn't a trade unionist. I'll tell you what I am. I am a preacher of discontent. I want to make you feel what wretched creatures you are. I want to make you say that you won't stand it. Trade unions are too slow for me; and they'll have nothing to do with such as most of you. The only hope for you is in shaking the classes with the mighty voice of your complaining.'

Jacob Dean was no doubt an unreasonable man. He wanted to solve the old problems of existence by some *tour de force*. He was a reformer in a hurry, who had not sufficiently considered the means of reform. He talked vaguely of 'the revolution.' His leading idea was that society must speedily pass through some topsy-turvy process.

Yet he was not a mere demagogue, for he was sincere. His ideas were crude, formless, the result rather of feeling than of thought, but there was no man living who was less of a sham. He worked hard at his trade of house-carpenter, and he never took a penny from those among whom, in his own phrase, he desired to organize discontent into a living force. Pity had in his mind taken the direction of a fierce hatred to the prosperous classes, that was all.

Yet nobody who looked at Jacob Dean would have taken him to be the author of those speeches some strong portions of which were occasionally quoted in hostile newspapers. There was certainly no misery in his face. On the contrary, he seemed to be the embodiment of good health, good temper, and high spirits. He had a fresh, bright-looking countenance, set in a frame of black hair and whiskers. His voice had as cheerful a ring as that of a prosperous farmer on market-day. He was altogether a manly sort of man, with a splendid physique, a rough, hearty, bustling way, and, withal, an intelligence more than usually cultivated and alert.

Jacob Dean was unlikely to do anything

that would bring him within reach of the law, yet he was probably as dangerous a man as was then in London. He was terribly in earnest, for one thing. He had convinced himself that all the evil of the world arose from the unequal distribution of wealth. If one man had got what other needy men wanted, then, according to Jacob Dean, his plain duty was to share his possessions with 'the workers.'

Of what are called constitutional methods of reform Jacob was angrily disdainful. The processes were too slow for his impetuous mind. What he wanted to see was a change in the whole social condition in his own lifetime, and in as small as possible a portion of that. He believed that there would some day soon be a great uprising of the working classes against those who, as he put it in his speeches, exploited the labourer; and that was what he was openly working for, but without having clearly defined to himself what amount of violence it might be necessary to employ. He was in favour of all strikes of workmen, for whatever cause —not because he believed that strikes were good in themselves, but because each one might bring somewhat nearer that momentous conflict of which he dreamed.

A man of this kind, if he have command of such a rough, powerful eloquence as that of Jacob Dean, is a great force for good or for evil; and the influence of this man, who worked hard at his trade, and who never took a penny for his addresses or lectures, was growing every day.

The public—by which phrase is meant in this instance that section of the public which Jacob was in the habit of describing as the indolent classes—has two ways of accounting for men like this. They are mere demagogues, greedy of power, and in love with their own voices; or they are men who have brooded too bitterly over what they have fancied to be their own wrongs. Jacob Dean belonged to neither category. He cared for power only for the sake of what it might achieve, and he had never had any wrongs that it was worth while to speak of.

His had been a very humdrum sort of life until the last few years. The most exciting episode had been the mysterious marriage of his sister, and the subsequent disappearance of her husband. Next in interest came his own marriage and the death of his wife—an event which, it must be admitted, he did not very deeply regret.

Jacob Dean had led to the altar that very Jane Ann Sayers who had been his sister's companion in her Crystal Palace adventure. He had not fallen in love, but had been entrapped by one whom he had first detested, then tolerated, and then begun to like because he had been able to do her a kindness.

Had he known what part Jane Ann had played in his sister's love affair he would have kept himself out of the reach of entanglement; but that was not revealed to him until after marriage, when the story was employed as one of a great variety of means for making him angry and miserable.

Jane Ann Sayers had set her cap at Jacob Dean when no other hope was left. He, poor fellow, was easily caught. He was a busy workman and a hard student. He had sought no female company. Wedded life had not presented itself to him in any other aspect than as a possible convenience, and it seemed natural enough to him that he should drift into marriage with Jane Ann Sayers.

She had expected to marry well, not to say splendidly, as do the heroines of all the penny serials; but her personal attractions had not proved equal to her ambition, and she was glad to get even a workman at last. However, it was no part of her plan to make such a husband happy. She exasperated Jacob with airs of superiority, made it appear that she had rejected wonderfully prosperous matches solely on his account, was slatternly of habit, and shrewish of tongue.

'There never was a woman,' said Jacob, 'who had so many ways of tormenting a man.' But, as was remarked previously, his experience of women had been limited.

When Jane Ann died the event was rather a relief than an occasion of deep and permanent sorrow. There was matter for more real grief in the fact that the one child she had left behind her was crippled and deformed.

To Jacob's energetic and practical mind a question often presented itself as to whether the child's mental peculiarities were not more to be deplored than her bodily defects.

'Nelly has the poetic temperament,' Brother Joshua would explain. 'The divine afflaytus runs in the family, my dear Jacob. You must see that for yourself. Of course, we don't all possess it alike. It falls upon me, for instance, and it skips over you, and then it falls upon little Nelly again.'

'The divine afflaytus be hanged!' said Jacob. 'A nice helpless fool it has made of you! If you want my opinion, it is that one poet in a family is just one too many, Brother Joshua.'

'Your words are harder than you mean to make 'em, I am sure they are, Jacob; so I won't resent 'em as I might. As for little Nelly, she's a poet, I tell you, which is something that you must make your mind up to, and that you cannot alter.'

Whether her uncle Joshua's explanation of Nelly's peculiarities was sound or not, it is certain that she was something quite incomprehensible to her father, who loved her none the less, however, because of the anxiety and mental perturbation of which she was the unconscious cause.

It was a fortunate thing for the child that, having lost her mother, such a good little woman as her aunt Bessie lived next door. During her father's long absences she spent most of her time in her aunt Bessie's house. There she made an idol of Bertie, and, as she dreamed much in the waking state, he became the central figure of her dreams.

'And the prince,' she would say, 'rode up to the castle, and blew a great blast on his horn; and then the castle gates flew open. After that the horse bounded into the courtyard, and when he raised his visor I saw that the prince was you.'

'I wish you would make-believe in other things than castles and princes,' Bertie more than once remarked. 'How you came to be such a little aristocrat I can't tell.'

'Princes are so nice, you know,' Nelly would respond. 'I wish you were a real prince, instead of being only a prince in my dreams. I am sure you would make a very good one, you great big Bertie.'

Then the lad would break out into denunciation of princes and great people generally; for Bertie Shelburne admired his uncle Jacob to the point of sharing all his opinions, and his ideas of the upper classes were, it must be admitted, shockingly depraved.

Day after day Nelly Dean sat in the big armchair by her aunt Bessie's window, and walked into dreamland with her eyes open.

What amazing romances she contrived to weave out of her bewildered imaginings! There was an uncommonly large brain behind her passionate dark eyes—a brain morbid and confused, but with a certain magical quality, which transformed whatever was poor and common into something great and splendid. Nelly's imagination was moulded upon the large scale, indeed.

Through the little back window at Peppermint Hill a branch of laburnum could be seen blossoming in its due season. It told of some hidden garden enclosed within jealous walls. Nelly would count the weeks and the months until this branch might be expected to burst into flower. This great event was her annually recurring miracle.

The sight of the yellow blossoms carried her straight into fairyland; and this was one of the dreams that the golden curls of the laburnum awakened: She beheld a garden, luxuriant and well-ordered, with flowers blossoming everywhere, and fountains flashing in a rosy light. Gorgeous butterflies flitted to and fro, themselves like living flowers. In a sunny part of this enchanted garden, half hidden by blossoms of wondrous perfume, a beautiful maiden lay asleep. That this was a princess Nelly knew at once, and then it dawned upon her more slowly that this princess was herself, in the likeness that she would wear in the world to which she really belonged, so different to the one in which she found herself when her dreams were over. Birds sang marvellously. There was a flutter of wings in the air, and by-and-by a trumpet was blown; then the princess moved on her arm, her eyes slowly opened, and as she became more fully awake she perceived a great company of knights winding down one of the pathways among the trees, and at their head there rode one who was splendidly attired; and he it was who, bidding the others pause, dismounted from his steed, doffed his plumed hat, and then bounded forward to fall at the princess's feet.

It was Bertie again—always Bertie. However magnificent the prince might be, he had always the same form and features, and was but a transformed image of one who would come home a few hours hence dressed in his coarse workman's clothes, with the grime of a day's labour on his face.

In little Nelly Dean the woman's nature was developing too early, forced into premature growth through suffering, and warmed in the hot-house of her wayward fancies. That sentimentalism which in the case of her mother had made one of the miseries of her father's brief married life had been inherited by the child in finer form, and was accompanied by a more passionate temperament and a vastly wider sweep of the imagination.

All which was a trouble to Jacob Dean. He persuaded himself that he might change the temper of her mind by a wise choice of books. He was particularly careful that she should remain a stranger to that class of literature in which his wife had sought for intellectual nourishment; but he was himself a reader of Scott and of Shakespeare, and so it happened that these had become her familiars at an age when Jacob Dean would have deemed them to be entirely beyond her comprehension.

What a wide field for her adventurous spirit to explore! She was each one of Shakespeare's heroines in turn. She lived, and loved, and suffered and made merry with them all. Now and again, too, they all trooped with her into her ideal world, and her fancy was luxuriantly fed by what practical Jacob Dean would have considered safe reading.

There were some of Nelly's day-dreams the nature of which nobody, not even Bertie Shelburne, guessed. Nelly would have died of shame if they had done so. Her aunt Bessie, who had a sweet, innocent meaning for everything, had convinced herself, on no grounds which could have been clearly stated, that the mind of the poor child dwelt chiefly on heavenly things. She must be thinking, said Bessie to herself, of the crown which the angels were keeping for her against the time when her cross should be laid down.

And all the while it was earthly and not heavenly love for which the woman-soul in the child-body was longing; and from love of that kind her affliction had shut her out for ever.

Never, surely, was so strange a nature dropped into such inapt surroundings! Uncle Joshua had such an explanation of the case as became a poet.

'Sometimes the fairies steal away little folks like you,' he observed to Nelly one day. 'But you were a fairy to begin with, you know; and you were left behind once, when there was a sudden flight, because you had fallen down and hurt yourself, and you couldn't run. That's how I account for things. Oh! by the way,' Uncle Joshua went on, 'I've been writing some poetry about you. I'm always writing poetry, you know. There's good sense in this, too. Listen:

> '"When visions strange and fancies deep
> Distract the head of Nelly Dean,
> She should, before she goes to sleep,
> Take some of Smith's Aurora-vine."

Now, what do you think of that for poetry, Nelly?'

And Nelly, disturbed by the sound of words to which she had not consciously listened, slowly withdrew herself from the bright world of her imagination.

CHAPTER IX.

AN ADVENTURE IN THE PARK.

THE parks were looking their best. The spring sunshine poured through the young leafage, and grass and gravel walks were alike dappled with intricate shadows. The earlier blossoming shrubs had burgeoned out into masses of bloom. There was the carol of birds in the air; innumerable quick-darting finches were twittering to each other, and the deep-throated thrush sent its voice out of many a leafy covert.

Surely, London is the greenest, the most rural of all the cities of the world. 'O wise and prudent John Bull!' some intelligent foreigner has observed, ' to ennoble thy metropolis with such spacious country walks, and to sweeten it with so much country air!' There are days when you may lie down on the grass and fancy that the city in which you slept last night has strangely cast you forth into some rural solitude, remote from men. The living stream of Piccadilly pours tumultuously along not far away, but its sounds are as the noise of a torrent pouring through moss-grown crevices in the bosom of a wood. How artificial is life just beyond the railings there, above the brow of the Marble Arch! How aboriginal it is here among the trees, on the grass, with the long, sweeping shadows of the clouds playing hide-and-seek over the wide green spaces!

Not all Londoners are aware of what glorious possessions they have in the parks. There are thousands who 'have never been so far.' They live no further away than the Borough, it may be; and there the Walworth Road offers itself, and the Sunday tram. Or they crowd contentedly into the slums of Spitalfields, where there are no fields left, not so much as a foot of grass-covered soil. Or they herd together down Stepney way, where they have forests of their own in the crowded masts of the India Docks. Man the Explorer is not born in the slums. His childhood must have been disturbed by the mystery of country lanes, leading who knows where, ere there awakens a thirst for travel within his breast.

Bertie Shelburne was a Londoner of another sort. He was gravely curious about the mighty city in which he lived. For one so young he had concerned himself much with its problems. He loved its pleasantness also. The parks he had only visited on Sundays or holiday seasons, when they did not wear their customary aspect, and were given over to the populace. However, for once in a way, there had befallen a holiday in which all the world did not share. Some important piece of machinery had broken down at the works, and for a day, or it might be two, Bertie was at liberty to enjoy himself as he pleased.

It was a piece of unexpected good fortune, and, after making Nelly Dean very happy for awhile, and keeping her from her dreams, he took a tramcar from Clapham to Vauxhall Bridge. Thence he crossed the river on foot, wandered through a dismal street in Westminster, lingered round the Abbey and the Houses of Parliament, and eventually found himself in St. James's Park. Thenceforth he was led by accident and curiosity, rather than by design. He watched the children and the nursemaids feeding the water-fowl; he gazed with interest, but without admiration, at the sentry in front of Buckingham Palace; he wandered through the Green Park, where there was an unexpected flock of sheep, 'feeding like one'; he crossed Piccadilly, entered Hyde Park, and, without knowing what gay sight it was that he beheld, found himself leaning over the railing and gazing at the splendours of Rotten Row at the full height of the season.

What a strange, brilliant scene it appeared to be to this youth, whose life was spent between the workshop in Pimlico and the cottage at Peppermint Hill! A tall, proud-looking, heavily-bearded man of full habit rode by, and there was a general lifting of hats.

'You didn't salute his lordship,' said a small, well-brushed, keen-eyed man, who was standing beside Bertie. 'P'raps ye didn't know 'm?' he added, transfixing the youth with his eye-glass.

'Know whom?' inquired Bertie.

'I thought you couldn't know 'm. Lord Sawbridgeworth, man alive! That's him wid the broad shoulders, riding ahead yander. See all the people ducking their hats to him, by way of respectful divarsion?'

The little man spoke with a terrible brogue, yet with the air of one who was neither ignorant nor ill-bred, and who had a decided inclination to be affable.

'And so that's Lord Sawbridgeworth?' Bertie observed. 'Thank you for telling me; but I shouldn't have lifted my hat even if I had known.'

'Not one of his party, eh, my young cockolorum? Well, small blame to ye, then! I'm not one of that sort myself, ayther; but when I meet a jintleman of his lordship's aisy manners, sorry I'd be not to do him the honour of liftin' my hat. It's not much of society ye'll be after seeing,' the little Irish gentleman added, after performing a few more salutes to persons in the Row.

'I see none at all,' replied Bertie. 'I am a workman; and if I were not a workman I should have nothing friendly to say to society, for I am a Socialist.'

'The divil y' are! It'll be a quare long time before that will do you anny good, let me tell ye! Do ye know what place this is, now—this very piece of gravel that ye're lookin' on?'

Bertie had to admit his ignorance.

'It's Rotten Row, bedad! And all those that are ridin' along it are them, and such as them, as the likes of you are thinkin' to upset. There's the Duke of Downshire, now—him wud the hat that's too big for him. He'll be a quare one to deal wud; and there's the Marquis of Flamingay'—another doff of the hat—' who'll give some trouble before he shares out aquil with you and me, I'm thinkin'.'

Bertie Shelburne would have argued the question of Socialism readily enough at another time. But the suggestion that the privileged world, with which his own dim under-world had to contend, was now parading before his eyes sent him off into long trains of thought, with the consequence that he lost many of the bright, but perhaps not strictly veracious, observations of his lively Milesian acquaintance.

And these were 'the classes'? What a blithe and *debonnaire* life they led! It was to all appearance very beautiful. The sight of it awakened all manner of new thoughts and longings. How easy, how pleasant, how sunny an existence was this, contrasted with the oil and grime of the machine-shop, contrasted with the small, cramped-up comforts of Peppermint Hill, contrasted with the inferno of acre on acre of London slums!

'How lucky it is,' Bertie almost unconsciously observed to himself, 'that the poor so seldom crowd to witness the recreations of the rich!'

He was thinking what might happen if a great mob of starving people should surge into the Park on a day like this, to witness such a display of triumphant and contented wealth. His rapid fancy pictured a wild uprising, howls, dismay, slaughter; and, oddly enough, he saw himself in front of the mob, not as a leader in the attack, but as an excited, energetic, half-maddened opponent of violence.

Saturated throughout with Jacob Dean's teaching, Bertie Shelburne never doubted that the scene before him owed all its brilliancy to the unjust sharing of the profits of labour. The lion's share had gone to the idle and the useless, and here, he concluded, the idle and the useless were all gathered together, contending with each other in ostentation.

Which was not just. In Lancashire the single brief phrase 'Awe maks' has a great power of expression; it signifies a conglomeration of everything. A Lancashire man would say that he had seen 'awe maks' of people in Rotten Row, and to a great extent he would be right. Noblemen, Cabinet Ministers, philanthropists, financiers, soldiers, popular divines, mere clubmen and Piccadilly loungers were all here together, and to a careless observation were all pretty

much alike. Here and there a figure stood
out from the rest.

There, for instance, was a great statesman,
who was daily anathematized by his enemies,
much as if he combined the qualities of
Richard III. and of that diabolical hero of
modern fiction, Edward Hyde. Bertie
Shelburne took him to be a very harmless-
looking, interesting old man, who would
have shone the better in such company for
a new coat.

There was the too pronouncedly beautiful
respondent in a celebrated divorce case.
Bertie's new Irish acquaintance insisted
that he should take note of this lady.

'Bedad, an' there she goes,' he said,
nudging the young man and recalling him
from his reverie. 'There's a fine woman
for you, annyhow!'

And a fine woman she was, undoubtedly,
in the large, affluent sense. Her riant,
sensuous face had been alike her ruin and
her fortune, for she had won a coronet by

losing her reputation. She played for high stakes, and won them.

'That,' said the small Irishman, pointing to a stately figure on horseback, 'is the Marquis of Carabas. He's had a dale of luck; the Lord help us! a power of luck indade.'

Bertie's eyes, following the Irishman's finger, fell upon a trio of equestrians. What a contrast two of them presented to the woman who had just passed! Here, at least, was purity, white and unsullied.

There was a high-bred look about the group, in the gentleman no less than in the ladies by whom he was accompanied.

'Them's the daughters of the Juke of Dundridge,' the obliging Irishman observed. 'Fine gyurls they are too; divilish fine gyurls, upon my worrud!' And he took off his hat as if he were an old acquaintance.

Other voices rose in comment.

'That is the Marquis of Carabas. Lucky

young beggar, eh? Made his mark in the House of Commons, taken into the Ministry, succeeded to his cousin quite unexpectedly, and now is going to marry Lady Ermyntrude Challoner, a last season's beauty, and the proudest woman in England.'

'Rather too proud for my taste,' said another voice in reply. 'I prefer more life, more go, more *chic*, more human nature, in short. A fellow doesn't want to marry a marble woman, however faultless the statue may be.'

All this as the little group passed ambling by. The other, younger lady, who appeared to Bertie Shelburne to be a mere child, was riding a tall raw-boned chestnut, an ugly-looking brute, which neither answered well to the curb nor seemed to enjoy the snail's pace of progress necessary in the Row. Now and again the rider stooped to caress the great creature, and to soothe it into quietude, but with very indifferent success.

'Why will you bring that ill-conditioned

Irish brute here, Nora?' Bertie heard the gentleman ask, and the reply came with the merriest laugh that had ever fallen on the young man's ears.

'Because I'm fond of him, to be sure. Poor dear old Thady! You and I have had many a happy time together, haven't we, although naughty people do call you ugly?'

They moved out of hearing almost at once, but the words, and the looks, and above all the glad youthful laugh, of Lady Nora Challoner had made an impression on Bertie Shelburne that he did not as yet understand. He leaned forward, and followed the group with his eyes until it was lost in the confused panorama of the Row.

Would such a bright creature as this, he wondered, ever be tamed down to the style of fashionable woman that seemed to be chiefly represented in the Park?

He turned the question over in his mind so earnestly that he was quite unconscious of the further comments of his Irish friend.

Suddenly there was a rush of people in his direction, and such a stir of excitement as showed that something unusual had occurred.

What was it?

The carriages had all moved on, and there was a comparatively open space of roadway in front of where Bertie stood. A salvo of shouts of consternation came towards him, and in an instant more a big horse came tearing along at a terrific pace.

The rider was a lady, and was evidently a magnificent horsewoman, as was seen by the way she kept her seat. Yet it was clear that something dreadful must occur ere long. It was impossible for her long to retain her seat.

Without taking a second for thought, Bertie Shelburne had vaulted over the railings. It was a critical moment. As the excited creature flew past he leapt at it with the spring of a young athlete, caught hold of the bridle, as it happened, and, after a tremendous shock, felt that he was being dragged along; felt also as if something had given way in his strong young wrist. It was but a brief struggle. The horse, more frightened than really vicious, came to a dead standstill, snorted, and then looked down as if reflecting on its own foolishness.

A number of men had clustered round, and one of these had assisted the rider to dismount.

'Oh, Thady,' she exclaimed, 'how could you treat me so!' And then Bertie saw that it was the youngest of the two ladies who had been accompanied by the Marquis of Carabas.

What had happened was this: The big Irish horse had been impatient of the pace of the Row, had fretted and chafed, and almost pulled Lady Nora's wrist off as she held it in. Then a dog ran across the gravel, and Thady, with his ears laid back mischievously, was off in a moment, tearing along like a whirlwind, and scattering all before him.

Lady Ermyntrude Challoner and the Marquis of Carabas rode up to the trembling heroine of the disaster almost as soon as that young lady had dismounted. Lady Nora had not fainted, and did not mean to faint. On the contrary, her cheeks were already recovering their normal hue.

'I am not hurt—not a bit—so don't bother, Ermy,' she said, in response to anxious inquiries. 'But that brave young man! Oh, Ermy, where is he? Will nobody thank him for me? He risked his life to save mine, you know.'

Lady Ermyntrude turned to where Bertie Shelburne was standing, back from the crowd, looking very white and stern.

'We are indeed greatly indebted to you for your splendid and ready courage,' she said, in her most gracious tones. 'It was a most heroic act, and probably you have saved my sister's life.'

It was not in human nature to be anything but pleased with such a speech, if it had only been delivered with a little less stiffness; but Lady Ermyntrude seemed to be consciously stooping from her high estate to acknowledge a favour from an inferior.

Bertie felt confused and a little vexed. He had no experience to guide him as to his behaviour in such circumstances as these, and in consequence he appeared at his very worst, awkward and ungracious.

'It was nothing,' he said, in a quick, abrupt sort of way. 'Somebody else would have done it if I hadn't.'

'That is not so certain as you seem to think, my brave young fellow,' said the Marquis of Carabas, coming to the side of Lady Ermyntrude, now that her sister was found to be so evidently uninjured.

'A working youth,' he said to himself. 'One may certainly offer him something, and put an end to further obligations.'

His hand went to his breast-pocket, and Bertie guessed for what reason. The look that mounted to his face was so eminently threatening and disdainful that on glancing at him again the Marquis of Carabas changed his intentions, and, instead of taking bank-notes from his pocket-book, he produced a card.

'It will be impossible to thank you now as you deserve,' he said. 'I am the Marquis of Carabas, as this card will tell you. If you will call upon me there is no reasonable service that you may not ask me to perform.'

Bertie was growing unreasonably angry.

'I want nothing,' he said. 'What I did was for the sake of common humanity, and I don't wish to be paid for it. I don't even want so much as thanks. I only want to be left alone.'

This ungracious speech was concluded with a spasm of wounded pride. The young fellow was in truth suffering both in mind and body, for his wrist was exquisitely painful. How he wished they would all go away and leave him!

That wish had changed an instant later. For the Lady Nora came up and looked at him gratefully and pityingly.

'Oh,' she said, 'you are hurt!' And Bertie thought that he saw tears in her eyes. 'We are all worrying you when we ought to be doing something for you! Oh, you are hurt very much, I am sure!' and she gave a little scream, as Bertie suddenly grasped the seat by which he was standing, as if he must otherwise have fallen.

'It is only my wrist,' he said, with a quick look of thanks for her thoughtfulness. 'I have sprained it, I think; that is all.'

She looked round anxiously, and suddenly her face lightened. An elderly gentleman stepped forward and raised his hat.

'Can I be of any service, Lady Nora?' he asked.

'Oh, I am sure you can, Dr. Poinsett. You are the very person we want. How fortunate it is that you are here!'

The doctor saw what was the matter at once. He took hold of Bertie's wrist, and the young fellow, feeling very sick and queer, was not sufficiently wrong-headed to refuse the examination.

'This is a case that I must take home with me,' said Dr. Poinsett. 'It is not serious, I assure you,' he said, in response to Lady Nora's anxious look; 'but it requires immediate attention. My carriage is quite near.'

'I'd not be doing my juty if I didn't see my young friend through his trouble; so I'll make bowld to ask you for a seat in your carriage, me dear doctor,' exclaimed the small Irishman, leaping in without further invitation. 'Me name's Delaney—Lawrence Octavius Delaney.'

Bertie Shelburne was too near fainting to explain that Mr. Delaney was no friend of his; and besides, it did not seem worth while. As they left the fashionable doctor's house shortly afterwards, the younger man with his hand bound up in splinters, the little Irishman observed :

'It's your fortune that's made, my young haro! it's " ask, and ye shall resave " with you, my chicken.'

'I shall ask nothing,' said Bertie. 'Those people don't even know my name, and they never shall know it. I want nothing. I want nobody's charity.'

'A mighty proud stomach ye've got, any way,' Mr. Delaney observed ; and then to himself, 'He'll ask for nothing, won't he? Then, bedad, I'll ask for a good dale on his behalf—and my own. It isn't often Dame Forchune puts such a chance in your way, Delaney, me bhoy! Ye'd be mighty to blame if ye didn't make the best of it this toime.'

CHAPTER X.

JACOB DEAN SUSPECTS A MYSTERY.

The daily miracle of the sunset transacts itself for all the world. The same fiery globe which buries itself in the western ocean, and flames behind Skiddaw, and empurples the summit of Ben Venue, on many a night makes the skies glorious above Peppermint Hill. There was a soft and quiet and gracious sunset on the night of Bertie Shelburne's adventure, with a sky compounded of indescribable gradations of pale primrose and green tints. Nelly Dean watched the colours flushing and fading, as she sat at the little window at 10, Magnolia Street; and out of the thin wisps of cloud here and there she formed landscapes for the scenery of her dreams.

Meantime, Bessie Shelburne was busily engaged in ironing her son's shirts—those snowy white shirts which were sacred to Sundays and to his indifferently-fitting suit of broadcloth.

No words passed between the woman who was so much of a child and the child who was so much of a woman. What were two such queerly contrasted creatures to talk about? As a matter of fact they seldom did talk; yet the same unromantic being whom each, according to her character, had clothed in romance, occupied their thoughts.

It was getting late for Bertie Shelburne to return home, but his mother felt no uneasiness about him. He had probably made a long walking excursion into the country, to put to its best use an unexpected holiday. He would come home tired, no doubt, but full of health and mirth and high spirits, as his wont was. So at least thought Bessie Shelburne, his mother.

Nelly Dean, when the sunlight had gone out of the sky, and the brightness had faded from her fancies, sighed to herself, 'Oh dear! what a long time that great Bertie is in coming.'

It was his custom to carry her home at night. With her, walking was almost an unknown exercise. She tried it sometimes, but only with the consequence of discovering afresh how really weak and ailing she was. But even if she had been twice as strong as she could ever hope to become she would still have wanted Bertie to carry her home, so accustomed a part of her life had that daily experience become.

And here he was at last. Nelly was the first to perceive his arrival as he opened the door at 10, Magnolia Street. But what had happened? Something dreadful, surely! Nelly gave a little scream when she saw the pallor of his face, and noticed that his right arm was in a sling.

'Oh, Bertie!' she cried, her small being palpitating with apprehension; 'what has happened to you, my darling little Bertie?'

She loved to call this strapping six-foot fellow by these loving diminutives.

And, of course, before Bertie could reply his mother had thrown herself upon him in a state of consternation, ready for tears.

'It is nothing,' he said—'only a little accident. There is nothing that requires to be done,' he continued, as he saw his mother instinctively preparing for some active line of conduct. 'I am splintered up and made all right, and there's an end of it.'

He sank down on a chair beside the hard horse-hair sofa on which Nelly sat. The little creature laid a soft hand upon his hair, and turned her great dark eyes upon him. She saw at once that something unusual and momentous had happened to her Bertie, in addition to any injury that he might have suffered. There was a new look on his face—a look not of mere bodily pain and weariness, but of some deep trouble of the soul.

'What has happened to you, my darling little Bertie?' she repeated; and meantime the mother's questions came in a flood.

It all seemed to poor Bertie but as a continuation of the annoyance that he had lately been undergoing.

What was there to tell? What was there to say? For almost the first time in his life he felt really cross with those who loved him. He wished now that he had stayed in some hospital until his fracture grew well. Among the causes of his vexation there was a half-savage, half-comic feeling that he must now be appearing in a rather melodramatic light. What he had done was so exactly the sort of thing that is done by the hero of a cheap novelette.

He answered questions with an unaccustomed surliness, but by dint of persistent questioning Bessie did at length succeed in obtaining some bare outline of the facts of the case. It follows as a matter of course that she at once elevated her son to the regulation heroic platform—a rickety and uncomfortable position for one whose dislike of any manner of 'showing off' was a matter both of personal modesty and of set determination.

There was nothing to make a fuss about, he vainly protested; why should anybody go on so about a trifle? The serious part of the affair was that he must be laid off work for a month or two, and that would be a costly business, as he did not belong to a union. There was more to say for the unions in such cases than Uncle Jacob appeared to have thought of.

Nelly had been stroking the injured arm as if it were a favourite cat. Here a suggestion of mischief presented itself to her.

'Perhaps,' she said, 'the young lady's friends will help you?'

Nothing more was needed to put to flight all that remained of Bertie Shelburne's moderate stock of patience.

'Who talks of help? who wants help?' he inquired, and he rose up and paced the little room angrily. 'Help is charity, and no charity shall ever enter this door while I am alive, at any rate!'

Nelly's unguarded suggestion had put a spark to a powder-magazine. He stormed and raged, to his mother's great amazement, and Bessie immediately turned her own feeble anger on Nelly Dean.

But Nelly cared nothing for any scolding just now. She had formed a little plan of her own: she proposed to test the extent of her power over this strong young cousin of hers; and also she meant to know more of the accident than had yet been told.

'Bertie,' she said, as the lad's mother left the room intent on some household cares, 'you are not good to me. How you do go on so at just a word or two! Come and sit down here, you great big cross boy. Now, tell me how it all was.'

Bertie's brief fury was past, and he felt repentant. She was so small and weak.

'Well,' he replied, for he had done just as she told him, being repaid by sundry caresses, 'it was just as it is in your fairy tales: the princess's horse ran away, and the disguised prince leaped over the Park railings and collared the bridle-rein, and then there was a rush and a scuffle, and, to finish all, a fairy doctor appeared on the scene and fastened up a wrist in splinters.'

It was easier, he found, to make fun of the affair than to put up with sympathy and condolence.

Nelly's great eyes were fixed upon his face in an eager, questioning fashion. Her ideal world had all faded away, and Bertie's new style of narration did not serve to recall it.

'Was she very beautiful—the princess —the—lady you rescued?' she asked, with a feeling as if some hand was gripping her heart.

Bertie coloured up at the question, but replied to it with what he meant to be raillery.

'Beautiful? I should think she was! Fairy princesses are always beautiful, aren't they?'

'Tell me about her face.'

'Oh, her face! you don't see much of the face of a princess when her horse is running away with her.'

'But she thanked you—you know she thanked you! and you saw more of her then.'

'Well, let me see; her face? Now, how would Uncle Josh describe it? We shall have Uncle Josh writing poetry on the subject, I suppose.'

'And what would Uncle Josh say about her face?' persisted Nelly. 'Bertie, you are afraid to tell me. You think what you will not say. What would Uncle Josh say?'

'He would say that it was like a spring morning, fresh and bright.'

Nelly asked no more questions; she fell back on the sofa wearily. A spring morning, fresh and bright. Her vivid imagination immediately realized the full force of the description, and she thought of herself with a dreary feeling of contrast—herself, a dreary, November-like existence, shadowy and indistinct.

Mrs. Shelburne was busy in making all manner of arrangements for her son's comfort. What a splendid boy he was! no mother ever had such a son! and the maternal bosom swelled with gratified pride. The idea had, however, presented itself to her that Bertie had been slighted by the object of his heroism. What else could account for his unwonted and capricious anger? When she came again into the little front room she talked aloud as she made work for her restlessly busy hands. But her words, which were of an enigmatic and puzzling description, seemed to be intended more for her own solace than for the hearing of Nelly and her son.

'And one as might be as good as them, after all,' said Bessie. 'Those as could speak might tell things if they cared! and he might hold up his head with the best of them, horses and carriages and all. Who knows?'

'What in the world are you running on about, mother?' Bertie inquired.

'I'm running on about you, to be sure, and about people as is too proud to be civil; and about——' But what else she was running on about was not then explained, for Jacob Dean entered, with a vigour about him, in spite of the toils of the day, like that of the north-east wind.

'Hollo! what's up?' he cried, noticing immediately Bertie's splintered and bandaged wrist.

Bertie explained matters briefly, and his mother elucidated—or at least expatiated

— with more fulness of detail. But Jacob had a talent for not listening to his sister's talk. It went in at one ear and out at the other, he said. To a man perfectly accustomed to accidents in the workshops and in house-building, Bertie's injured wrist did not present itself as a serious affair, and Jacob Dean's mind was just then full of other things. Leaving that subject altogether, therefore, he said to Bertie:

'I've been to the house of one of those young swells who have been fussing about our meetings lately. Says he's a Socialist. Rum sort of Socialist he seems to be. Calls his place " chambers," and has it furnished up to the knocker—pictures, pottery, goodness knows what!'

'And what could take you there?' Bertie inquired.

'Went on invitation, my lad. Important business, the young swell said. It seems that he wants to teach us what Socialism really is. Says we have got hold of the wrong end of the stick—only says it more grandly. You should just hear his jaw! Talked of "the mixed and inseparable elements of modern humanity," and so on. It was like a book, and probably it was a book—one of those that you can make nothing of.'

Then Jacob Dean burst into a hearty roar of laughter. He told how this dilettante Socialist had taken him into some special room where there was a light burning on a sort of altar, with a picture hung near to it as if it were an altar-piece.

'Didn't know what to make of the light at first,' said Jacob Dean. 'Came to the conclusion that it must be for the use of smokers. That seemed considerate. A man with a pipe can stand a good deal more jaw than a man who's only just listening. So I lighted up cheerfully enough, and you should have heard the shriek that the fellow gave! He threw himself on me as if he meant to fight, but he didn't make much of that. It seems that he is a Buddhist or something, and that the light is the thing to which he says his prayers. Rum idea, isn't it? There's no danger that I shall be invited to those chambers again. But here I am jawing away myself,' said Jacob, 'and it's past the little girl's bedtime. Must carry her in myself now, I suppose. By the way, what was the name of those people you were talking about?'

'The Marquis of Carabas, and Lady This and Lady That,' said Nelly, before the youth had time to speak. 'Just think of Bertie making the acquaintance of such folk!'

'The Marquis of Carabas? I know something about him. Pretends to be a friend of the working man: wants their votes for his party. Just wait a minute, and I'll look him up.'

Jacob Dean hurried into his own house, and returned a minute afterwards with a thick, dumpy-looking book in his hands.

'Just look at that,' he said to Bertie. 'That's a book, if you like!—Carpenter's

"Peerage for the People." They're very scarce now. The peers bought 'em all up, I suppose. Tells too much truth about 'em. Look at this picture — a crown tilted so as to make a rat-trap, and baited with titles.'

'Hadn't we better go home, father?' Nelly inquired.

'Just wait a minute, lass. I want to look up this Marquis of Carabas; it will tell all about him here. You may find his whole pedigree in this; it's given here, and it will be given in Burke. You'd find a wonderful difference between 'em, I've no doubt.'

'That's curious,' Jacob went on, as he referred to the book : ' " Marquis of Carabas —family name, Shelburne; motto in Latin —free translation, 'Look after yourself.' " Nothing curious in that. But I say, Bessie, family name, Shelburne—what do you make out of that?'

'What do you expect me to make of it,

Jacob?' asked Bessie. 'There must be plenty of Shelburnes in the world.'

'There was no finding one when we wanted him,' said Jacob Dean. 'But the names are what they call a coincidence, I suppose. Let us see what else Carpenter says. "Title of eldest son, Lord Bexley."'

Bessie gave a little gasp, and turned away to dust the cheap mahogany sideboard with her apron.

'Something in it, is there?' said Jacob to himself. He thrust the book into his pocket. 'We'll be going, Nelly,' he said, and took the ailing girl up in his arms. She cast a sad, longing, and yet angry look at Bertie, and resigned herself unwillingly to his substitute.

'It is for the sake of the lady who is like a spring day that he cannot carry me to-night,' she murmured to herself. 'Oh, I shall never, never forget that!'

When Jacob Dean reached the door he paused, with his light burden in his arms.

'I have somewhat to say to you, Bessie,' he observed. 'I'll come back in half an hour or so, when you get that youngster comfortably settled in bed.'

Bessie started as if she had been shot. Her mind flew to some letters that had been hidden upstairs for many years past. And now there was an explanation to come! Well, it had to come some time. It might be best to put things straight—for Bertie's sake.

CHAPTER XI.

A FAMILY HIGHLY CONNECTED.

Alas, poor Nelly Dean! She was lying awake with tear-bestrewn cheeks and a throbbing brain. Her day-dreams would never again be as pleasant as they had been. An unexpected hand had interposed itself, and torn up the web of her fancies, which now seemed to hang in ragged fragments all around her, with the hard face of her everyday life looking through.

'A little, ugly, lame thing! that is what I am,' said Nelly, 'and not a princess at all.'

Her quick imagination had woven all

manner of possibilities out of Bertie's bare narrative of the incident in the Park. Even her mother's novel-fed fancy could not have bounded along at a swifter pace.

'A little, lame, ugly girl, whom no one cares about, who can win pity only, and must never hope for love.' So she moaned on, the dismal truth never having presented itself until now.

'Oh Bertie, Bertie, Bertie! And you are lost to me — you whom I fondly reckoned on as my very own; and there is nothing pleasant left for me in all the world.'

Such a mind as Nelly Dean's is an instrument of self-torture. Nelly was spared no single pang that a genius for believing in the improbable could inflict. Her cousin Bertie, in whose manly strength and comeliness she had delighted, had turned away from her, and fallen in love with a lady who rode in the Park— a lady who was the daughter of a Duke.

It was all very well for him to declare that he had scarcely seen her, but he must have noticed her very closely indeed, or how did he come to describe her as a young girl who looked like a spring day?

The careless phrase rankled in the little creature's too susceptible heart until it became poisonous. She attached a thousand significations to it that Bertie, when he employed it, never dreamed of. She conjured up visions of beauty and grace, exquisite features and symmetrical proportions, which were certainly as entirely opposite to Lady Nora's *nez retroussé* and short, strong figure as could well be imagined.

Perhaps, after all, the morbid mind of Nelly found a certain satisfaction in the misery these visions caused her. At every fresh beauty added by her luxuriant fancy to her unconscious rival, a new pang shot through her heart; yet such agonies as these, she felt, were better than quiet, dull, tearless silence.

'But she is the daughter of a Duke—a real live Duke, and Bertie is only a working engineer, that is one consolation!' mused the little creature, in an effort to console herself. Then she broke into sobs and cried herself to sleep.

In the meantime, and quite unconscious of the tragedy upstairs, Jacob Dean had returned to the house of his sister, where he sat down in the arm-chair by the fire and took out his pipe.

'How is the young un now?' he inquired, in what seemed a voice of unconcern. It was part of his plan of life to seem much more stoical than he really was. As a matter of fact, he was as fond of Bertie as if the lad had been a son of his own.

And now he was proud of him, too. The youngster had shown pluck, which, to Jacob Dean's mind, was almost the highest virtue. 'But the mother can be silly enough without any help of mine,' he reflected. 'There's no chance that this feat will be made too little of, anyhow!'

Bessie replied to his question very dolefully.

'He's not able to sleep yet,' she said. 'I'm feared his wrist pains him sadly, though he won't let on to it a bit, he's so brave.'

'Oh, he'll be all right soon enough,' said Jacob. 'He doesn't want to be mollycoddled and made a fuss over, you take my word for it. Not him! You women beat everything for making a fuss about trifles.'

'Oh, how can you speak like that, Jacob? A trifle, indeed! He saved a lady's life, anyhow; I'm sure he did. And there, his poor wrist is broken! and I'd sooner every bone in my body had been broke;' and here Bessie resorted to the comfort of tears.

'You've no heart for your own kin, Jacob,' she sobbed out; 'and brave lad as he is, too, such as any uncle might be proud of!'

'Brave fiddlesticks!' said Jacob; 'why, such things as that are being done every day, woman. What does stopping a runaway horse amount to? If he'd been that fireman, now, that saved the poor woman in the next street the other day, one would have had reason to brag of him. But to stop a runaway horse—why, Bessie, you might have done it yourself almost!'

'If he'd been *your* lad 'stead of *mine* you would have looked at it differently,' said Bessie, with a shade of offence in her tone.

Jacob leaned forward and patted his sister on the shoulder. 'Now, now, lass, you know you're saying what you don't believe! But let that pass. If needs be I'll stick to the lad through thick and thin; first, because he *is* yours, and second, because he's a fine and a whole-hearted youngster, and I love him.'

'Ah, now you speak like yourself, Jacob Dean, and as if you had a heart in your body,' said the mother, drying her tears.

'By the way, Bessie,' observed Jacob, coming to the subject which had brought him in again to-night, 'here's that book that I was telling you about—that which tells all about the Marquis of Carabas, you know.'

'Well, Jacob?'

Bessie's face assumed a look of pain and apprehension.

'Now, Bessie, isn't it a bit odd that the name of the Marquis of Carabas should be the same as yours?'

'There are lots of Shelburnes in the world. You once said that yourself, Jacob. You know you did!'

'I dare say! But here's another odd thing. The last Marquis of Carabas—he was only the Marquis for a month or two—left England just about the time when that husband of yours cut away.'

'And what can he have to do with me, or with Bertie?' the mother inquired. 'What had we to do with Marquises until yesterday?'

'That's just what I'm trying to find out,' Jacob said. 'Things come about in a curious way sometimes.'

He smoked his pipe in silence for a-while, casting his dark piercing eyes upon his sister now and then.

'I'll tell you what I've begun to think, Bessie,' he said at length: 'you haven't told me all you know about that blackguard, confound him! I mean that husband of yours. What is it that you are keeping back?'

Bessie's face grew pale and red by turns. She hung down her head as if she had done something shameful. It was in little, half-angry, half-timid gasps that she said at length:

'I don't know as I kept anything back as concerns you, Jacob. What if I have a few letters? They are my own. They are all I have belonging to him. And I never thought of them till years after he had gone —indeed I didn't.'

'Letters, eh? Just bring those letters

here. A nice woman for trusting those near to you, you are! Hides things from her own brother, it seems.'

'Why do you speak to me like that?' Bessie whimpered—'as if I had done something ever so wrong,' she cried. 'If I have kept anything back, it was because they might have taken the boy from me. Oh, I felt sure they would. And I *knew* nothing at all, whatever I might have suspected. You ought not to look at me and talk to me like that, Jacob.'

Jacob laughed rather grimly.

'Common-sense and women-folk are always far apart, it seems. So you kept your lad out of the way of claiming his birthright lest you might lose him altogether. And yet they say mothers are unselfish.'

'How dare you say as I am selfish!' broke out the mother with a sudden flame of anger. 'If it could do him good, you know I would willingly be cut into little pieces.'

'I dare say! But that is not the point. You have deceived me, Bessie. I shall find it hard to believe you again. Let us have no more nonsense now. You have some papers—letters, eh?'

'It is only a bundle of letters as once fell out of his pocket when I was brushing his coat, and that I forgot to give back to him until it was too late — until I had lost him for good.'

'Well, bring them to me. Your husband has left you to get on as you liked, or as you could. We have a right to all the information those letters can give us.'

'I never read them, Jacob, never! I did not think it honourable. I always meant to give them back; and, indeed, I forgot them altogether till years afterward, when they turned up in a drawer I was clearing out. And they are his, you know. I don't know as I ought to let you have them. If he came back and wanted them, what should I say to him, Jacob?'

'Say? Say you gave them to me,' returned Jacob immediately.

He could have laughed at the trusting folly and undying hopefulness of his sister; but there was a touch of pathos about it that restrained him, hard and practical as he was.

Bessie went to her little workbox, and, unlocking it, produced the bundle of letters, rapidly yellowing with age. Her own hand trembled as she placed them in his. It was a moment fraught with destiny. What revelation was awaiting her? What influence upon her life, and upon the life of her boy, would such revelation have?

'Why, these are addressed to "Lord Bexley"!' remarked Jacob, with a look of eager inquiry.

Then he took up his book again, and examined still more closely the entry relating to the Marquis of Carabas.

He had half-forgotten the formal-looking lines which preceded the family history, and one of these was the most important just now.

'Eldest son, Lord Bexley!' he exclaimed under his breath. Then aloud: 'Why, it's as plain as mud in a wineglass, Bessie, my lass! Your husband was the man who disappeared, and who was murdered in Alaska. Your husband was, in very truth, the last Marquis of Carabas!'

Bessie looked up, her eyes growing round and big like those of a frightened child. And so this was what was meant by the name on the letters, which had puzzled her heretofore. Her husband was the Lord Bexley to whom they were addressed!

'Then Jane Ann was right, after all!' she said with a tremulous sort of laugh. 'I always thought she made those romances of hers up, and that such things couldn't take place in real life. A real live Marquis married to me—me, poor little Bessie Dean, whom nobody set much store by! Why, Jacob, it's—it's really too ridic'lous!'

'Good Lord! what fools women are!' said Jacob. 'And that's how it strikes her——'

He rose up and paced the floor, uncertain whether to be angry or to laugh outright, for he had caught Bessie in the act of looking at herself in the mirror over the mantelpiece.

It was a pleasant and comely face that was reflected back to her, in spite of its crow's-feet and growing wrinkles, but, as seen with its shabby setting of cap and linen collar, was certainly very inappropriate considered as the face of one who might belong to the British aristocracy.

It was, indeed, emphatically the face of a woman of the working classes — homely, respectable, commonplace, *bourgeoise* to a degree.

What a Marchioness of Carabas ought to have resembled was shadowed forth very faintly in the imagination of Bessie Shelburne; but of this at least she was certain, no characteristic of her own visage ought to be found in the looks of so great a lady.

Bessie was a childish, ignorant, rudimentary creature at the best, and her moods were wont to be uncertain and capricious. The mingled pride and mirth evoked by the ludicrous nature of the situation passed quickly away, and was followed by a queer, wistful contraction of the muscles of her face, which became like the face of a child just before it cries. The burden of an honour to which she was not born began to press heavily upon her moral consciousness.

To Jacob's further amazement, she sat down suddenly and, throwing her apron over her face, burst into heartrending sobs.

'What on earth—why, Bessie, lass, is there anything to take on about in what I have said? You women beat everything for queerness! We've just found out that you are a Marchioness or something, and, bless me, if here you are not crying as though your heart would break!'

'Oh, Jacob, it's too ridic'lous!' was all the explanation vouchsafed through this hurricane of weeping.

There was a great deal more taking place in Bessie's mind just then than Jacob would have given her credit for thinking and feeling. First, there was the humiliating thought that the man she had loved should have so sedulously deceived her. Then there was the relief at perils past—said perils taking the form of society and its demands upon a poor, timid, untutored mind. Last of all, a peculiar sort of pathetic pride in the fact that he, so great by birth, should have stooped to love her at all—a consideration sufficient to draw tears from feminine eyes at any time.

Besides—and this last was the most powerful factor in the tears, after all—she had at length grasped the one great feature of the case which had at first escaped her. The man she had loved so unselfishly was dead.

Never until that moment had she realized

how strong was still within her breast the hope of seeing him again. Always she had dreamed that he would return some day and tell her of his sorrow for deserting her; that he would beg for her forgiveness, and that they might still grow old together, as true lovers ought. She would then show him the boy—their boy—and ask with trembling pride if she had not done her duty by him; if he had not grown up straight, manly, honest, and handsome.

And now it could never be! That dream was over.

'Oh, and he is dead—dead! I shall never see him more!' sobbed Bessie; 'and I have never put on so much as a bit of crêpe!'

'Look here, Bessie,' exclaimed Jacob, utterly bewildered by this feminine behaviour, 'don't you say a word of this to anybody, most of all not to the lad! And now good-night!

'Well, I'm jiggered!' he muttered to himself as he opened his own door; 'if it doesn't beat creation for strangeness! The Dean family connected by marriage with the aristocracy! *That* won't help the cause if it's ever known.!'

CHAPTER XII.

BESSIE PUTS ON MOURNING.

In the quiet of his own house Jacob Dean sat down to think of the course of events. But first of all, 'to pull his mind together,' as he said to himself, he took up his 'Peerage for the People,' and read all over again the two or three pages which were devoted to the ancestors of the Marquis of Carabas. The writer had set himself the task of bringing together all the ugly facts of the family history. There was nothing particularly black or revolting. One of the Shelburnes had been involved a century ago in a scandal with a woman; several had held profitable sinecure offices under the

Crown, and all had been tolerably successful in providing for the younger members of the family through the various departments.

'Tax-eaters, every man of them!' reflected Jacob Dean.

He had a really genuine detestation of aristocracy. It was not the mere hatred of the poor man to the rich—he wanted for himself nothing that anybody else possessed; but he had seen terrible misery—had been accustomed to see little else, in fact—and he believed that the rich and idle were devouring the patrimony of the poor.

As he sat staring into the dying fire, the 'Peerage for the People'—it was but a shabby volume—fell from his knees to the floor, and these things shaped themselves in his mind:

There could be no doubt that Bessie's son was the true Marquis of Carabas. The identity between that Marquis who, according to the newspapers, had perished in Alaska, and the man who had married and then deserted his sister, was conclusively established by the letters that Bessie had for so many years been hiding away. Bexley was the title of the eldest son of the Marquis of Carabas—so the 'Peerage for the People' stated—and when that unfortunate marriage took place the old Marquis was still alive, so that his son could be no more than Lord Bexley. Then the present Marquis had succeeded in default of direct heirs; yet there was a true heir alive, a workman, the nephew of Jacob Dean the Socialist, Bertie Shelburne, Adelbert—for he bore a favourite family name, the name of his father, as it would appear—and he was lying upstairs, next door, suffering from an injury that he had received in doing service to some female acquaintance of the so-called Marquis of Carabas.

It was clear enough to Jacob Dean that by a very easy manner of proceeding he could create an extraordinary flutter in aristocratic circles. To proclaim a workman as the Marquis of Carabas—to reduce a great nobleman to the position of a commoner—to seat a young Socialist in the House of Lords! In the way of sensations nothing could go much beyond that.

But as he recounted these possibilities Jacob Dean became aware that there was that in him which would forbid a single step towards their realization, at least on his own part. When he asked Bessie to be silent on the subject, he was scarcely aware of why he made the request; but the more he thought the matter over, the more he felt it would be a violation of all his own theories to try to alter what seemed to have been satisfactorily settled by accident.

The idea of self-interest never entered his mind. He did not consider for a moment that if Bertie Shelburne became the Marquis of Carabas Jacob Dean, the workman, would probably be made very prosperous.

'All one has to think of,' he observed to himself, 'is what is best for the lad. He's comfortable enough as he is, and he's contented enough. It cannot be best to unsettle him. To make him into a lord would be likely enough to make him what other lords are. The best thing, decidedly, is to make a man of him, and there's plenty of good stuff to work on there, I think.'

Why not altogether ignore this surprising discovery? Why not leave the lad to mature into a noble, hard-working manhood, to dignify a class to which he believed himself to belong, rather than to alarm and scandalize a class to which he really belonged by right of descent?

Jacob asked himself questions of this kind in all manner of forms; and, though he felt that Bertie himself should have the right to choose, he finally determined to withhold that right of choice, at least for a time, if Bessie could be persuaded to keep her mouth closed upon the same subject.

But there was much danger in regard to

Bessie, as speedily appeared. She was determined to indulge herself in all outward and visible signs of widowhood. It appeared to her simple comprehension that in wearing colours through all those years of loneliness and desertion she had defrauded the man whom she had loved of what was his just due. There was something positively revolting in the thought. The decencies and solemnities of mourning are sacred things in the class to which Bessie belonged. There is a genuine solace for these wounded and bereaved souls in tucks of crêpe and voluminous black veils.

Jacob was made fully aware of this disturbing fact on the very next occasion on which he visited the house next door. Bessie was dressed in black merino, with folds of crêpe, and had a white cap on her head, that unmistakable widow's badge, with flying streamers to the rear. For a moment Jacob wondered who it could be that she was in mourning for.

'Bless my soul, woman !' he said, 'what does this mean ?'

'Why, what should it mean, Jacob,' asked Bessie, whimpering, 'except that I have put on the proper mourning for my husband, as is dead ?'

'Mourning be hanged! He never deserved that any woman should mourn for him, least of all after he has been dead so long. Look here, Bessie——'

Jacob Dean crossed the little room to make sure that the door leading to the stairs was tightly closed.

'Has the lad seen you in these things ?' he resumed.

'No,' said Bessie; 'they have only just come from the dressmaker's. I hadn't time to make them myself, so I got a young girl I know to do them for me. And the cap I bought down Lambeth way, and cheap it was at five shillings !'

'Or Joshua ?'

'No, nor Joshua either.'

'Then just go and take them off at once, and I'll be back in half an hour's time. Now, no nonsense, mind! I have reasons for what I ask you to do.'

As he closed the door behind him Bessie whimpered more, but was half inclined to revolt against his authority.

'Our Jacob takes too much upon him,' she said to herself, 'and I don't know as it's proper for me to give in to him as much as I have done. I'm sure I don't.'

But it was only a little flicker of rebellion; and she did, in fact, just as she had been told to do.

The truth was that this adoption of mourning had been a very serious matter indeed with Bessie. She had never thought so long and so seriously about anything as about this, with the one exception of that husband who had made her life what it was. Not that there was much substance in her thoughts. How could there be, seeing what sort of creature she had been made?

The predominant idea in her mind when Jacob had unfolded the tale which he had based on his 'Peerage for the People' was that she had done a great wrong to her husband's memory. She had not mourned for him as a respectable woman should. Why, if this was true she was a widow—had been a widow for years, and knew it not. Where were her weeds, her insignia of woe? What disrespect had she not unwittingly shown to his dear memory by this lapse of etiquette, this disregard for the decencies of widowhood! Her tears fell fast as all these questions arose to trouble her peace of mind. All she had borne from the man was forgotten. He was dead, and she had not mourned him. This was all she could realize. To a woman like Bessie there was something almost indecent in the fact that she had flaunted abroad in colours while her husband lay in a grave in alien soil. Depth of crêpe means depth of respect to such as she.

Ay, it was hard of Jacob to deprive her of a solace which was also an atonement; yet when he entered the little parlour again she was dressed in her usual homely garb.

'I have been thinking all this matter over,' he said, as he sat down in a chair, at the same time motioning to her to sit down beside him. 'I must smoke as I talk about it to you, or I shall lose my patience, I know. Can you keep a secret, Bessie?'

'What secret, Jacob?'

'Why, this secret—about that blackguard husband of yours; about what we believe the lad to be; about the folk in this house being in any way different to the neighbours.'

Bessie waited a few moments before she spoke. Her mind was partly suspicious and partly bewildered. The revolt against Jacob was rising fast.

'Why should we keep it secret, Jacob?' she asked.

'That's just what I want to make you

understand. I've thought it all over from top to bottom, Bessie.'

'But that isn't thinking it over for me.'

'Yes it is. It is thinking it over for all of us. We are all bound up together. What is for the good of one is for the good of all. Look here, Bessie'—and he laid his hand on her plump little arm—'Bertie is more to us than he can be to anybody else.'

'He is more to me. He is more to me than all the world beside. If I were to lose him—if that accident were to——' She broke out into a passion of sobbing, as if she were apprehensive of some immediate calamity.

Jacob waited very patiently, with his hand laid comfortingly on her arm. He was conscious of unusual tenderness and pity; but also he was aware that if his point was to be gained he must soothe and mollify her, coaxing rather than bending her to his will.

'There's nothing of that kind to fear,' he

said, as the sobs quieted down a little. 'It is not of losing him in that way that you should be thinking. The accident is nothing. He will be out to-morrow; he will be at work again after his arm has had a week or two of rest. But look here, Bessie. Suppose I am right—suppose that your husband was the man I take him to have been; don't you see that Bertie doesn't belong to us—doesn't belong to you, even—but to rank and fortune and great people?'

'How could it ever happen that he doesn't belong to me, Jacob? I bore him, I nursed him, I have slaved for him; he has been more than my life to me all these years. I am his mother, Jacob—oh yes, I am his mother; and whatever his father may have been, he is my own lad—he is my son!'

It was a difficult matter to argue, Jacob Dean felt; and he had a settled conviction, too, that women are not amenable to argument. It was necessary to get Bessie's feelings and her motherly doubts and fears on his side.

'I want to put it to you this way, Bessie,' he proceeded to say. 'If Bertie's father was Lord Bexley, who should have become Marquis of Carabas—and I haven't the least doubt on that subject, for those letters of yours seem to make it quite clear—then what have we to look forward to? If his relatives claim him, they are certain to object to you. They will place barriers between you; they will take care that you shall come together as little as may be. They will——'

But here Jacob was interrupted by a half-stifled scream. His sister's eyes glanced up at him in terror, round as the eyes of a startled owl. The battle for secrecy was half won.

'You couldn't bear separation—that is plain to see,' Jacob went on. 'And what have we to look at on the other side? If these great folks don't own him—as very likely they won't, being rascals mostly—and he should set up a claim of his own, we shall either be ruined by lawsuits, the lot of us, or he will be set down by everybody as an impostor should he make such a pretension without going to law.'

It was evident from the look of Bessie's face that she was not following her brother any longer; he had gone beyond her depth. Even the impression previously made was weakened. Jacob saw that he must adopt a simpler and more direct style.

'Look at the case of the Tichborne Claimant,' he said. 'You remember all about that, don't you?'

'Not very well now, Jacob. Tell me how it was.'

'Well, the Tichborne Claimant went away when he was a young man, and was drowned at sea, folks said. But ever so many years afterwards he turned up again and claimed his estates. There was no end of law, first in this court and then in that, and the end of it all was that the Tichborne Claimant found himself in gaol. That's what comes of claiming titles and estates.'

'Oh, oh, oh!' sobbed Bessie, 'was there ever such trouble in the world? Why didn't I burn those letters years and years ago?'

'There need be no trouble at all,' said Jacob. 'Trouble meets those that go to fetch it, Bessie. Keep a quiet tongue in your head, and it will never come to you.'

'What is it as you want me to do, Jacob?'

'Just to behave as you have always done; just to be yourself; just to think nothing about who Bertie's father was, or who Bertie may be. That's all.'

'And mustn't I let even Bertie know?'

'Why should you unsettle the lad? He is a brave, manly chap. He is content enough to be what he has always been. We shall all come to be proud of him some day, I can tell you—far prouder than we should ever be if you turned his mind from us to think of these other things.'

The mother's heart was soothed greatly by this praise of her son.

'You were always wiser than me, Jacob,' she said. 'You have thought and fended for all of us. I will do just what you tell me, dear.'

'Well, then, that's settled. All I ask you is to say nothing to anybody about what we have been talking about, or what we believe to be true.'

'And if Bertie should come to know some day, and should blame me for what I have done—oh, it would break my heart, Jacob!'

'He is too good a lad to blame you, Bessie, for doing what you believe to be for his good. Trust it all to me. If it is ever best for him to know, he shall be told. And now good-night; and, be sure, never a word!'

Jacob felt the victory to be complete;

and as he turned to leave he put his arm round his sister's waist and kissed her on the forehead. He had not performed so tender an act for years past.

'And may I wear my mourning, Jacob?' she asked, as he placed his hand on the latch of the door.

'Why, bless the woman!' he said, turning round again, 'that would spoil everything! We should have all the fat in the fire at once.'

Bessie began to whimper again. The new mourning weeds lay close at her heart. She wanted to experience the luxury of real widowhood. Jacob saw that the point was serious, and he sat down again. It struck him that she might desire to wear the mourning rather for her own satisfaction than for the sake of making a show before the neighbours.

'Let's see what can be done,' he said, taking her hand in his. 'You want to feel that you are doing right to that black— well, to your husband's memory.'

'That's just it, Jacob.'

'Well, you needn't always wear the mourning, you know. You might wear it a bit sometimes; I don't see why you shouldn't. Only don't let anybody see it, that's all. Wear it upstairs, you know, when there's nobody with you to look on.'

The simple idea captivated Bessie's child-like fancy. She saw herself seated before her glass, arranging the material of her black dress and the crêpe folds of her bonnet. The luxury of mourning might be all the greater if it were enjoyed in secret.

'Very well, Jacob,' she said; 'I will.'

CHAPTER XIII.

SURPRISING FAILURES OF MEMORY.

Bertie Shelburne had much reason to be grateful for the accident which had, for the time being, disabled his arm, and he knew it. The two or three weeks during which he remained away from work became the most fruitful period of his life. He had worked hard in a vast workshop, among rough men, from his fourteenth year. He liked his work well enough, but also he had a love of reading and a thirst for information that were altogether incapable of being satisfied by such opportunities of study as presented themselves when each day's work was done.

A curious phenomenon is frequently to be observed in working-men who read, and who pass among their mates as 'very larned chaps, mind you.' They really do get to know a great deal, in a rough and tumble sort of way. They read serious books generally, but without a definite purpose. They have to find their way among books by rule of thumb. One author makes favourable mention of another, and they go to the free library, if there be one in their neighbourhood, to make acquaintance with the writer who has just been brought before their notice. If there is no free library, they go to some second-hand shop and hunt for what they want in the fourpenny box; or they will save up small sums for week after week in order to buy some edition that they have seen in a bookseller's window.

They wander into the dark lanes and *culs-de-sac* of literature for lack of guidance. A workman who desired to study natural history saved up his pocket-money for many months on end, and then purchased Goldsmith's 'Animated Nature' secondhand, in four large volumes, and he read that work with absorbed interest, never becoming aware, till years afterwards, that he had, in the main, thrown his time and money away.

The result of such reading is not cultivation. The old, solid ignorance remains, though here and there a patch of learned veneer may be visible. It is very pitiable. There are thousands of eager readers who take no polish from reading: they never acquire the power of speaking correctly; they develop self-conceit, but are incapable of culture.

Here and there may be found a workman who, seeking a way for himself, hits upon the right one. He becomes genuinely cultivated without being helped by any of the ordinary means of cultivation; he adds taste and discrimination to the mere thirst for knowledge, and he is therefore one of those who make their way in the world. It was to this small and select class that Bertie Shelburne belonged. His reading not merely informed, but refined him; he was as incapable of resisting the influences of culture as most of his fellow-workers were of absorbing them. And now the injury to his arm positively did him a good turn, in keeping him at home awhile, and thus supplying him with wider opportunities of reading than he had ever had in his life before. It was, after all, a blessed thing—this slight accident that he had himself encountered in averting injury from another.

His intervals of recreation were spent with Nelly or Uncle Josh. He had never observed either of them so minutely before. He had accepted them as a natural part of his surroundings, heartily liking them both —loving little Nelly in a brotherly way, even—but never greatly noticing their peculiarities. The discovery that they were both phenomenal, both out of the common, followed quickly enough on a closer observance of their ways.

'Uncle Josh, you should be doing something better than writing quack advertisements in rhyme,' he said one day when his uncle looked up from his work, as haggard as if he had been labouring on an epic.

'Eh, what's that you say, lad?'

'You should do something better than this puffing of quack medicines.'

'And so I am doing something better, Bertie: I have been engaged to make verses for a hatter in the Borough and an umbrella-maker in the City.'

'Oh, nonsense! that's not what I mean, Uncle Josh. If you are really a poet, it is absolutely shameful in you to do these things.'

'I know it is, Bertie, my lad; I know it is.'

He flicked his handkerchief across his face. There were actually tears in his eyes.

Then Bertie, with a sudden pang of

remorse, remembered that Joshua had been helping his mother very considerably out of the pitiful earnings gained as rhymester to tradesmen and vendors of quack medicines. What a cruel injustice that he should have forgotten this! And he had just twitted Uncle Josh about his sordid devotion to filthy lucre. His face flamed with honest shame.

'Uncle Josh,' he said with genuine emotion, 'you ought to pound me for my stupidity and cheek. But, indeed, it was more stupidity than impudence. I forgot how good you had been to mother since I was laid by. By God! I ought to have said it was a grand and heroic thing of you to write those trumpery versicles, instead of laughing at you for it. Forgive me, Uncle Josh!'

'Don't say another word, lad,' returned the poet, the tears now distinctly perceptible in his watery blue eyes; 'you couldn't guess what a pleasure it has been to be able to help somebody—at last; me, that everyone has looked down upon and jeered at for a wastrel and a dreamer. Why, Bertie, it—it has made me feel like a man, not an incumbrance, as I felt before.'

Even then Bertie did not know the extent of his obligation to Uncle Josh. The poet had given up to the family need the dream of his life. These silent heroisms are going on around us every day, but nobody guesses them. The money for which he had—as he fancied—prostituted his genius, was meant in time to earn him recognition and fame. He intended, in short, to save a sufficient sum from what he had made in this mean fashion to publish at his own expense a selection of his poetry —a modest volume bound in cloth, with gilt lettering, and perhaps a flower sprawling across the cover. That little book had formed the principal item in all his visions, day and night, for long past, and now it had had to be banished for ever.

But all this he carefully kept buried in his own breast, and demanded no recognition of the sacrifice.

'I have taken farewell of poetry,' he said. '"She found me poor, and kept me so," as a greater poet has remarked. I can live by writing these rhymes; and I must live, even if I am a poet, you know.'

'You are getting quite practical-minded, Uncle Josh,' Bertie observed. 'The influence of the new sort of work, I suppose? But I fancy it is for our sakes, not your own. And so you have taken farewell of poetry for good. That had to be done in rhyme too, I expect?'

'Oh yes; in verse. One must take farewell of the Muse in verse. See, here are some of the lines. Tell me what you think of them:

> '"Oh, Poesy, thou spirit fair and free,
>   Whom I have followed for these many years,
> Not to be worshipped but on bended knee,
>   Not to be won save by long prayers and tears."'

'But you do usually worship on bended

knee, don't you, Uncle Josh?' He had not even yet brought himself to regard his uncle's gift quite seriously.

Uncle Josh proceeded without noticing the interruption:

> ' " The world is hard and eager, bears no Nay,
>   The meagre body's frail, and must be fed;
> O Poesy, thou art not for to-day,
>   And none behold the nimbus round thine head.' "

'That's first-rate, Uncle Josh. At least, it's ever so much better than that "Aurora-vine" stuff that you have been hammering away at. But why bid farewell to poetry at all? Why not start on a new line, and become the poet of the people?'

A light shot into Joshua Dean's eyes for a moment, but then the old hopeless look came back again.

'The people don't want any poets,' he said. 'They don't understand them.'

'Oh yes, they do, if the poets can make themselves understood. But the best of them won't, and those who do make themselves intelligible produce poetry and water.

There's chance enough for you, Uncle Josh, if you can sing the songs of the new democracy.'

'Put Jacob's ideas in verse, you mean?'

'Well, something like that.'

'It's a good notion, lad. It would be a grand thing to write a new "Marseillaise"—something that a whole populace would sing, that would fire men's hearts in the struggle for freedom.'

'That is just the idea, Uncle Josh. It is a poet like that who is really wanted in these days.'

'But how are the people to be reached? There's the old difficulty of publishing, you see.'

'Publish on sheets, and sell the sheets at a penny each. Let whatever you do be written to some well-known air. It is in that way that the people are to be reached. Publish your twopenny-halfpenny books, and they will never hear of them. Give them a sheet, with something to sing upon it, set to a tune, and there you are. There's both money and fame in it, Uncle Josh, and there's great possibility of usefulness, too.'

Joshua Dean was becoming excited under the influence of the new suggestion. He passed his hands quickly through his ragged hair; his wits went wool-gathering; his eyes assumed that vacant stare which is an indication of looking inwards; and so Bertie left him, perceiving that no more could be profitably said.

It was afternoon, and Bertie had decided to give himself a rest, after days of hard labour at his books, but as to what to do with himself he was not quite clear in his mind. An unintentional suggestion came from Nelly Dean, whom he found curled up in the armchair of his mother's parlour, looking very lost and sad. The character of her dreams had changed; she did not sit at the window any more; she did not look out into fairyland. How beautiful was one who was as beautiful as a spring day? Such was the question that troubled her. No day was so wondrously fair—spring, or summer, or autumn—at Peppermint Hill. But there must be beautiful days where the flowers came from; and the flowers began to come in spring. How perfect must have been the lady whom Bertie had rescued; and surely he would not have spoken like that if she had not won his heart?

It was impossible for this small creature to live in any but a self-created world. She had previously lived in a world of happiness; now she lived in a world of despair. But the first keen pangs of jealousy had given way to a drear hopelessness, in which she longed for Bertie's presence as much as ever, though he seemed to stick pins into her forlorn being when they were together. He sat down by her now on the stool at her feet.

'Well,' he said, 'where has my little lady's imagination been careering to this time? Among fairies or griffins or mighty enchanters?'

'Oh, I don't dream of those things now. All my dreams have gone out, just as one blows out a candle.'

'Why, that seems very odd! Are you not unhappy without them?'

'Something does make me unhappy. But don't let us talk of such things now. Let us talk about you, Bertie.'

'With all my heart, little woman! But what is there to be said about me?'

'I have thought so very much about that lady whom you saved.'

'Have you indeed? Why, I had almost forgotten all about her!'

A gleam of pleased surprise shot over Nelly's face.

'Don't you think that when you were hurt in saving her she ought to have come to ask how you were?'

'How could she come, you silly thing? She does not even know who I am. Besides, such people don't come ; they send. Generally they send a creature in plush, I believe. If such a fellow were to come asking about me, I think I should kick him.'

If Bertie had never said who he was and where he lived, if he had almost forgotten the lady who was as fair as a spring day, what had Nelly Dean to fear? Her heart revived as she asked these questions of herself. She began to look and to talk as of old, and she and Bertie said many foolish things to each other, all about the world of make-believe, the gate of which seemed to be opening once more to that restless and fervid imagination.

But Nelly's talk had decided Bertie as to what he should do with the remainder of the long summer's day. He would go to Hyde Park. He knew nothing of the habits of the aristocracy. He had an idea that they drove about Rotten Row all day when the weather was fine. Perhaps he might be able to see the girl to whom he had done a service, and in whose behalf he had sustained his hurt.

It was a great way to Hyde Park, but he arrived there long before the Row was deserted—while the loungers on seats and railings were still numerous, indeed. And what he had anticipated happened much in the order of his expectations, for before much time had passed there rode by the Marquis of Carabas, with Lady Nora and Lady Ermyntrude Challoner at his side.

Bertie, however, lost his opportunity for that time. He was like the poor man who watched for a thousand years before the gate of Paradise, and who succumbed at last to the power of sleep. Whilst he snatched that brief slumber, the gate opened and shut again, and he was outside for ever. Bertie, after gazing vainly and longingly down the drive, turned to look at an extraordinarily dressed woman, whose ultra-fashionable attire struck him with amazement; and during this short interval those for whom he had been watching passed on, by him unnoticed.

But directly afterwards he recognised them, and, craning his neck, watched them down the Row. Ah, well, they were there; that was something, at least. And perhaps they would return, after the manner of the rest of the folks who keep going round and round this fashionable inferno.

Yes; after a little longer time of patient watching he saw them again advancing towards him, and, pushing his way to the front, he waited his time. Would they— would *she* recognise him?

He told himself that he was an idiot to imagine such a thing as probable, but he hoped for it all the same. When he tried to convince himself that she would behave as his preconceived notions of the aristocracy led him to expect, the remembrance of her honest eyes and frank manner gave the lie to his old ideas. Nevertheless, when they got close to him Lady Nora, who was riding on the nearer side, could not help but see him, and yet it appeared as though she would have fain been blind.

A gleam of recognition shot into those honest eyes of which he had been dreaming, and she started violently. Then all at once a great rush of colour swept over her face, and she turned away and said something to the Marquis of Carabas.

He, for his part, glanced at once in Bertie's direction; but there was no kindliness in the glance—nothing but a cold, hard, haughty indifference that froze the young blood in the lad's veins for a moment, and then made it surge rebelliously to his forehead.

He clenched his fist involuntarily.

'I hate that fellow!' he muttered. 'I think I hated him from the first moment I saw him almost. If I believed in fate and all that sort of rubbish, as mother does, I should begin to fancy we were born to do each other a mortal injury. But I don't think it's that. It's just that we hate each other instinctively, like a rat and a terrier. But I did think *she* was different. I'll never believe in a face again—nor a voice, either, for that matter.'

The whole thing stunned him for a moment. He had come there expecting nothing—at the most led by a hope that he might see, as it passed, a face that had influenced him more powerfully than any face which he had yet beheld. He had not himself wished to be seen or known; but surely, since without doubt he had been seen, he deserved some recognition other than what seemed like an expression of contempt.

'But it is what I might have expected, after all,' he said to himself. 'They are aristocrats, and I am a workman. If they had behaved differently, what right should I have to think as I do of their class? It is a good thing that this has happened. It is a good thing for me. It saves me. It proves that Uncle Jacob's teaching is all right. I did a service at the peril of my life, but I belong to an inferior order of men, and must not expect gratitude from such as they. I should be a fool to expect it. And yet half an hour ago I would have done anything almost for a smile from that lovely face. Which shows that I am a fool, without question.'

In this unpleasant mood, without distinct purpose, and almost without volition, Bertie pursued the route taken by the Marquis of Carabas and his companions. He saw them alight from their horses. A man stood waiting by the gate, as if he had been expecting their appearance. Between him and the Marquis a few words passed. The latter took something from his pocket and handed it to the man, who then walked away.

'I seem to know that fellow,' said Bertie; and he stepped forward a little more quickly to overtake him. 'Why,' he went on, as he got nearer, 'it's the Irishman that I was speaking to at the time of the accident. I owe him some thanks. He went with me to the doctor's, I remember. Hi!'

The Irishman looked round, glanced at Bertie, and then quickened his pace.

'Why, the fellow seems to be running away. Hi, there!' He hastened forward and placed his hand on the man's shoulder. 'Don't you remember me?' he asked.

'Never saw you before, faith. And hwhat do ye mane by calling out after a gintleman like that, now? Is it beggin' ye are, or hwhat? Sure, and ye'll get nothing from me. It's moinded to give ye in charrage I am.'

And with these words the Irishman resumed his rapid pace, leaving Bertie astounded at so surprising a lack of memory.

CHAPTER XIV.

A DUKE'S DAUGHTERS.

AND concerning the young lady whom Bertie Shelburne had saved from a shocking accident, or possibly a frightful death, and who had apparently made so complete a recovery from the sense of obligation?

Well, Lady Nora had been peremptorily forbidden to ride Thady again during her stay in town. Her mother, the Duchess of Dundridge, was quite firm on that subject, as on most other matters. The fact was, Lady Nora should have been still in the schoolroom, for she had not long entered on her seventeenth year. But she was a girl with a will of her own, and she had so pleaded, and so contrived, for a season in town and a taste of its gaieties, that she had eventually obtained what she longed for, precedent being waived for once in a way, as much the easiest manner of quieting a plague. The regulation début, the presentation, and all the rest, were to come in the following season. These were great events, to be anticipated with as much eagerness and disturbance of mind as if they involved, not the fortune of one young lady only, but that of the world. Meantime, there were quiet dances here and there, and pleasant little social functions that even one who was not a débutante might attend. Up to the time of that exciting incident in the Park, Lady Nora had shared in almost as much fun and enjoyment as she had ventured to look forward to.

There was one high matter concerning which it was not requisite that she should pass through any disturbance of mind, and it was one about which most girls, arrived at her time of life, would have been disturbed exceedingly.

The tender budding soul of a maid is apt to get excited about thoughts and affairs of love — to grow in love with loving, even before there has presented itself a fitting object of affection.

But on such subjects Lady Nora had neither dreams nor longings. That matter had been decided for her by her stern and unbending mamma, long ago. The Duchess of Dundridge had settled the fate of both of her daughters, equally to her satisfaction and, as it seemed for the present, to theirs.

Whether she was seen by 'anybody' or not Lady Nora did not care. It was a matter of no importance. She desired neither to catch nor to be caught, and on the subject by which young minds are most troubled and excited when they come to the point where womanhood and girlhood meet she was absolutely at ease.

Her sister, Lady Ermyntrude, was to

make a marriage of the splendid sort. That was no more than natural, seeing that she was a fashionable beauty, the eldest daughter of an ancient family, the feminine impersonation of the pride and hauteur of a dukedom.

As for 'little ugly Nora,' as she was wont to be called, it was arranged that she also should do passing well. So far back as in the days of short petticoats she had been contracted to her cousin, Lord Cranbery, and they had grown up together from childhood with an apparently clear understanding of their future relationship. Their courtship had, indeed, been pretty to see, chiefly because there was so little courtship in it, both parties taking it for granted that the arrangement made in their interest was a part of the special ordering of Providence, and acting accordingly.

Lord Cranbery was not rich, but it was also a libel on Lady Nora to say that she was ugly, as even the Duchess, who disapproved of her younger daughter's style, was fain to confess, with a certain wondering candour, now and again.

She was short and rather stoutly built; she was even inelegant, it may be; but she was the very incarnation of intense life. Her being throbbed with vitality, and she had the charm of all eager, observant, easily interested, bright and full natures.

As to her defects, what were they? Certainly her form was not classical; her pretty little nose had an unmistakable upward turn; her mouth was well shaped, but wide. Nevertheless, there were the prettiest and most bewitching dimples at the corner of this mouth when she laughed, as she was almost always doing. Her gray eyes were lively with fun and mischief; her complexion was of that adorable sort which the sun cannot spoil or the wind roughen, and her reddish-brown hair was touzled in short, merry curls.

Her accomplishments, it must be admitted, were of such a character as her stately mother abhorred. She could ride any horse bare-backed, and groom and saddle him if need be; she delighted in every sort of athletic exercise and outdoor recreation. For the rest, she was wild, impulsive, outspoken, and absolutely honest and truthful.

What the Duchess disapproved of in her character seemed to commend her all the more to her father's liking. From him she had inherited her love of animals and outdoor life. He made a pet and a confidante of her, and she was immeasurably tender and affectionate towards him.

The Duke of Dundridge was a plain man, of ruddy complexion, good-natured, easy of temper, careless of the distinctions of rank. He would have made an admirable gentleman-farmer had he been born to that position in life. As things were, he was strongly devoted to agricultural pursuits, was practically the steward of his own estates, and was proud of nothing so much as being president of the Agricultural Society of his county.

'The Duke would have made an excellent clodhopper,' said the Duchess, in one of her impatient moments; 'and I really think that Nora would be in a position ideally suited to her tastes if she were servant-girl on a farm. Thank God that Ermyntrude is so different!'

And certainly Lady Ermyntrude was in all respects the opposite of Lady Nora in tastes and character.

It was a subject of great regret to the energetic Duchess that fate had denied her the pleasure of giving to the world a son, an heir to the Dundridge estates and position.

And if only Lady Ermyntrude had been a boy, what a perfect successor to these she would have proved! Ambitious, clever, intellectual, with great social abilities, it appeared hard indeed that she should have to accept a subordinate position because of her sex.

Two or three mornings after the exciting event in the Park, Lady Ermyntrude Challoner was seated near one of the windows in her father's house in Park Lane. Her fingers were busy with a piece of elaborate embroidery, designed for the decoration of her favourite Ritualistic church, and meantime her mind revolved many things.

Before long she would become the Marchioness of Carabas. The position was one which she meant to fill with distinction. Her husband, already an eminent figure in the political world, should be urged forward until he filled the highest office in the State, and no inconsiderable part of his advancement he should owe to her, for she meant to be powerful with those who wielded power, and to influence Cabinets by means of evening parties.

The future lay before her clear and fair;

and for her lover she felt something almost approaching to real affection as she contemplated the possibilities of his position and career.

Lady Nora would have been puzzled and astonished had she known what thoughts were passing through her sister's mind. No serious thought as to the future had ever intruded itself on her own understanding. Why should it? Everything was decided for her beforehand, on a basis clearly satisfactory to all parties, even to her inconsiderate self. There was somewhat in her nature that had not yet begun to bud. Upon the physical side she was perfectly and splendidly developed, but the true soul slumbered as yet, its radiant wings still rudimentary and closely folded up.

Her restless vitality asserted itself to an uncomfortable extent when, as upon this particular morning, she was obliged to remain within doors.

Even the charming morning-room, with its artistic decorations, and pale salmon and gold judiciously blended, its dainty watercolours, graceful statuettes, and masses of spring flowers in bloom, felt to her like a prison, and she pined for fresher air, and teased Bonbon, her sister's toy spaniel, from mere impatience of monotony, and hailed with delight the arrival of her cousin and betrothed, Lord Cranbery, chiefly because he was such an admirable victim for raillery.

'Oh, I am so glad you are come, Cranbery!' she exclaimed, as she saluted him. 'I'm tired of town already. There are so many nuisances and restrictions in it. One mustn't go anywhere by one's self. One mustn't do this because other people don't, and one mustn't do that because everybody who isn't anybody does it, and—and one mustn't ride poor old Thady because the dear thing doesn't like walking like a mute at a funeral.'

'I should think not, indeed,' replied Lord

Cranbery, laughing. 'Surely you had sufficient of Thady on that last memorable occasion?'

'It wasn't his fault, the dear! It was all because of that stupid dog. And then people will be so disagreeable.'

'Who is disagreeable, Nora?'

'I know who is disturbing, at least,' murmured Lady Ermyntrude, stooping to untie her skein of floss-silk from the neck of Bonbon, where Nora had fastened it.

'*He* is. I mean the young man who stopped Thady from running away with me —at least, from running away too far,' amended Lady Nora; 'he refused to give Dr. Poinsett his address, and his poor wrist was broken, you know, and he would not be able to work, and — and we saw him the other day, and he looked so offended.'

Under all the girl's laughing pettishness there was a tone of genuine regret, that quite touched Lord Cranbery.

'Never mind, Nora,' he said gently; 'I

think Carabas has now done all that can be done. If the young fellow feels sore we cannot help it.'

'It is very annoying, certainly,' remarked Lady Ermyntrude, 'but we cannot accuse ourselves of ingratitude. The young man was — well, you understand, Cran, how stand-offish and rude those common people can be when they choose to think that one is patronizing?'

'I don't like the phrase common people, Ermy,' said the young nobleman gravely. 'It always brings to my mind St. Peter and his moral lesson : " What I have made, call not thou common or unclean."'

'Besides, he was not common—not a bit,' broke in Lady Nora indignantly ; 'you look at a man's coat, Ermy, and that is stupid. The tailor makes that.'

'I cannot congratulate your hero on his tailor, certainly, nor his bootmaker either, for that matter!'

'There! Didn't I say so? Just as

though it mattered! Badly-fitting coat or no, he looked simply splendid when he was telling Carabas that he was not a beggar, and did not require payment for what he had done. He looked, indeed—ah, yes, you saw it too, Ermy, though you are not likely to admit it!'

The girl's voice had sunk a little towards the end of the sentence, and she looked rather doubtfully at her beautiful sister. Lady Ermyntrude's face flushed slightly, but she kept her eyes fixed on her work.

'What was it that struck you as so curious?' asked Lord Cranbery, rather astonished at their significant expressions.

'Why this, Cran. When he raised his head and flashed that defiant glance at the Marquis, their two faces were so exceedingly alike. No, it was not only my excited imagination, I tell you, because Ermy saw it too. I read it in her eyes.'

'You read anything rather than your books, Nora,' remarked Lady Ermyntrude quietly. Then, with a sort of forced reluctance, she added: 'But Nora is right for once, Cran. There really was a sort of likeness; which is very humiliating.'

In Lady Ermyntrude's tone was such an unmistakable annoyance that neither her sister nor Lord Cranbery pursued the subject further.

Of all men, Cranbery seemed the least likely to win the love of a girl of Lady Nora's type.

He was a serious young man, who studied theology, and—his digestion; took serious views of life—and dinner-pills. He was rather fond of what his cousin had called common people, prided himself upon his breadth of view, though in reality Nature had unfitted him for breadth of any sort. He had frequently presided at meetings in Exeter Hall, and had even been known to preach to ballet girls and costermongers. In appearance he was thin, yellow, and bilious-looking.

Lady Nora reverted to her love for country pursuits upon leaving the theme obnoxious to her sister.

'Yet you were eager enough to come to town?' said Lady Ermyntrude.

'Yes, of course. One wants to do everything—everything! I love it all. Dancing, singing, riding, flirting. Well, you needn't frown, Cran; I give you leave to flirt in turn, if it amuses you! One wants to live, in short. But, after all, the country for me. I am like daddy. And daddy should have been born a farmer, if all things in this topsy-turvy world came right. Then I should have been a farmer's daughter, and what a jolly one I should have made! What prizes we'd have carried off between us for horthorns and for butter!'

'And what part should I have played in life?' asked Lord Cranbery, with condescending gravity. Listening to his cousin's chatter was to him very like watching a kitten at play.

'Oh, you? Let me see. Had you been born a Methodist you'd have made a capital local preacher. Or perhaps you might have rivalled " Koofah " if you'd given your mind to it !'

'Nora, how dreadfully reckless you are in your way of speaking!' said Lady Ermyntrude; 'and who *is* " Koofah," in the name of all that is marvellous ?'

'Marvellous enough, if you only knew, Ermy! "Koofah" is a very celebrated man—he is really! He makes the lame to walk and the blind to see. He pulls out teeth by magic. He has a grand gilded car, and Indian servants, and a brass band that never plays any other tune than " See the Conquering Hero comes." How very, very sick he must get of that tune! But never mind! It drowns the cries of the victims if they make any. He has invented a patent pill which, if taken in sufficient quantities (and there is a considerable reduction for quantities), is warranted to make old people young again. That is what I am always hoping will happen to Cranbery, because I bought him a box when we were down at Allerby, and he took them—all! Now, you needn't blush, Cran, you know you did!'

If there was one thing more seductive than another to Lord Cranbery, it was patent medicine.

Had he chosen, indeed, to lend the prestige of his name to the various compounds swallowed by him during the course of a year he could by this simple process have quadrupled his income.

It was quite true that he had been tempted by the flaming advertisement attached by the vendor to each box of pills, and had fallen a victim to the lure set for him by his merry cousin. They had made him exceedingly ill, and he had cursed the name of 'Koofah'—or, at least, had come as near to that unholy process as a truly pious young man could.

Alas that this experience taught him

nothing! He was quite as eager and ready now as then to become the subject of fresh experiments.

'I don't think you ought to laugh, Nora,' he said, with piteous indignation. 'You would not, if you knew what it was to suffer. Why, the whole of one's usefulness and happiness in life—nay, I will go further, and declare that the tone of one's moral philosophy is ruled by the state of one's digestion. You do not realize how completely the physical dominates the spiritual. It is indeed very, very difficult to take correct views when pain reigns supreme or the liver is out of order.'

'I thank goodness I never had an ache or a pain in my life. Not even the heartache, Cran—imagine that!'

'I don't believe you,' retorted the young nobleman stoutly. 'No one who is not entirely heartless could go through life, even so far as to arrive at the mature age of—seventeen is it, Nora?—without having an ache there. I don't mean love troubles, and that sort of imaginary thing,' went on Lord Cranbery with the sublime contempt of ignorance, 'but genuine heart-ache over the sins and the sufferings of this miserable world.'

A cloud passed over the bright face of the girl, and with an impatient exclamation she jumped up from her seat.

'It isn't a miserable world at all, Cran!' she cried; 'it's only the way you choose to look at it. I dare say your liver is wrong again, which accounts for your correct views. I don't believe in universal misery, and the world is very beautiful. If I see people sad I try to make them laugh, and that does them good. They find, perhaps, things are not so bad as they seem, after all. If they are poor I've always a shilling to give them.'

'Some people will not have your shillings,' said Lady Ermyntrude, with cold severity, 'however they need them. It is very amusing to hear you talk of life—you who have never known it—and of misery to be grinned into happiness. You are a mere child, Nora, and a very foolish and heedless one sometimes.'

'I'm sure I get lectures enough to make me wise,' pouted the girl.

But nothing could induce her to be serious. She danced round the room like an embodied sunbeam, and presently stopped before the mirror. It was a charming reflection that she saw there, and she smiled at it even while chiding it.

'Why, oh! why did nature not give me a grand presence like you, Ermy? You were the eldest, so you took all the good things. Am I not a strange little changeling to belong to a ducal house? Such a nose, too!' and she stroked the pretty little nasal organ with considerable tenderness. 'Never mind! It's not so bad when one gets used to it, and I shouldn't have liked to live in meek subjection to my nose—like the lady to her blue tea-pot—as I might have done had nature adorned me with a superb classic such as yours, Ermy. Cran dear, will you forgive me my nose and other infirmities if I allow you to swallow as many pills as your soul inclines to?'

'You are very vain, Nora, and I will not administer any food to your vanity,' was the calm response.

'Am I vain? Well, perhaps I am. At least, I am glad I've got a decent complexion and pretty eyes. But I'm wasted on you, Cran—clean and entirely wasted. Heigh-ho! what a mistake it all is! Why weren't we left alone to choose whom we liked, or to remain single had we been so minded? I have an idea that we shall be awfully miserable together, you and I. But let us laugh and make merry, and not meet trouble half-way.'

CHAPTER XV.

LORD CRANBERY MAKES AN ACQUAINTANCE.

LORD CRANBERY had called Lady Nora vain; but he also had his own special vanity.

He prided himself upon having developed his character in a thoroughly all-round manner. Every side of his nature, he heartily believed, had been carefully tended and cultivated after the methods inculcated by Cobbett and Smiles, until his faculties were as evenly balanced as a pair of scales. The rational, the emotional, the religious, the social, the physical, the spiritual, the imaginative, the artistic—each was in its due proportion to the other.

On the whole, the result was a trifle

disappointing to his friends, though he himself had for the present no misgivings. The limitations of his powers caused him no pang. He by no means yearned after larger powers.

But to other people it was an enigma as to wherein lay the benefit of culture so diffusive, especially when applied to talents of an essentially mediocre description. The tiny brook, which, confined within its narrow bed, runs along bright and rippling in the sunlight, is in nowise improved by being allowed to spread itself over a level tract and become a stagnant marsh.

But Cran was contented with small attainments and feeble triumphs. Good, conscientious, small-minded, he was perfectly happy in himself, and was consequently the envy of all the crowd of restless, unsatisfied folk who sneered at him openly, and secretly coveted his peace of mind.

He attended lectures, classes, reading circles, philanthropical meetings, art schools, science demonstrations, and musical 'at homes.'

Small wonder was it that his poor brain got somewhat muddled during the process of self-culture. It was while the artistic and imaginative side was under treatment that fate brought the young nobleman into contact with Mr. Zachary Luxmore.

This gentleman was the apostle of realistic devotional painting, a new and startling development in the world of art. Mr. Luxmore had certainly not 'awakened to find himself famous,' because he had taken care to keep very wide-awake indeed during the years of his pursuit of the fickle goddess Fortune. Like a successful stockbroker, he studied the markets, and eventually made a hit.

'I shall knock 'em some day,' he said to himself; and as he knew himself very well, the confident prediction was amply realized.

Who has not heard of Luxmore's 'Jael and Sisera,' of his 'Judith slaying Holofernes,' of his 'Herodias dancing before Herod'? Each of these great works was the picture of its year.

The success of Zachary Luxmore was founded on a careful study of the outrageous and the bizarre. The public had become tired of most things in art, most things having become tiresome, indeed. Realism—bare, hard, unsentimental, but very pretentious realism—was being done to death; and was becoming a bore, which was worse.

'We are living in a period of decadence,' moaned one of the great art teachers of the day. 'What is ugly is loved for its own sake. The sense of beauty has left us; we appreciate only the fetid, the ghastly, the corrupt. The true feelings of devotion to art and of devotion to God have perished together. There is no longer either greatness of subject or sincerity of treatment. A frightful unreality is dominating us under the name of the real. One searches our exhibitions in vain for a mind and a soul.'

Zachary Luxmore spoke contemptuously enough of the lecture in which these phrases appeared; but he went home full of a new idea. The sacred and the realistic! Why should they not be combined? A judicious blend meant a hit. All the devotional subjects had been painted; but not as he could paint them.

The Bible had been ransacked for these centuries past in the interests of the exhibition and the studio; but it might still be possible to ransack it to some new purpose.

'Hallo, Luxmore! have you turned recluse?' one of his friends inquired about a fortnight after the lecture. 'It seems to be weeks since I saw you at the club.'

'I have been working rather close,' was the reply.

'Got something big on hand?'

'I am just going to knock 'em next May, that's all.'

The acquaintance laughed as he told the story of this meeting to a group of the members of the Wampum Club. Luxmore was not a general favourite there, his self-confidence having hitherto been so vastly in excess of his achievement.

But the Biblical picture that should have nothing devotional in it, that should seem as real as a shop window in the Strand, that should at once appeal to the prevalent passion and to what the public would mistake for religious sentiment—that was the idea.

He would be realistic, without doubt, but not in the pre-Raphaelite style, exploded years ago. He would work in a much more modern and distinctly Parisian method.

And in May his 'Jael and Sisera' appeared on the Academy walls. It occasioned a perfect *furore* of enthusiasm amongst many who ought to have known better. His drawing was splendid indeed, and his technique unimpeachable, or he would never have dared what he had attempted.

It was astonishing how beautiful his work

appeared in the eyes of connoisseurs who had condemned the nude when considered simply as the nude; but here they had something of the sacred sort, and under such circumstances scanty raiment did not appear so immodest as in a work which was merely unpretentious and pure.

Luxmore was himself a small man, but the canvases upon which he worked were of Titanic dimensions. His Judiths, Susannas, and Deborahs, were scarce of lower altitude than the gigantic creations of Michael Angelo. He painted mountains of flesh as firm and ripe as Rubens' goddesses, and he succeeded amazingly. He was abused by some of the critics, no doubt, but all this helped his fame. His natural impudence, combined as it was with daring, and exceeding cleverness and mastery of technique, did wonders for him.

It was a strange sight to witness the little man at work, truly. A pigmy manufacturing giants.

Lord Cranbery was an intensely proper young man, and on his first acquaintance with it the fashionable artist's work shocked him considerably. But then he was told, by those who ought to know, that Luxmore had created an entirely new school of devotional art—one which, in real feeling, was to eclipse the Old Masters altogether. It was impressed upon him that, in fact, he was a sort of nineteenth-century Fra Lippo Lippi.

Numbers of people were ready to say these things, and if there were any who hesitated, Luxmore helped them out.

> 'I am bold to say
> I can do with my pencil what I know,
> What I see, what at the bottom of my heart
> I wish for, if I ever wish so deep—
> Do easily, too; when I say perfectly,
> I do not boast, perhaps. Yourself are judge.'

And so Cranbery was persuaded that the new painter of Biblical subjects had been born to revolutionize art, and to set it utterly free from conventions and puerilities.

The artist had—for an artist—a keen eye

to the main chance; and although Lord Cranbery was too poor to buy pictures, he was always made welcome at the studio, because he had a great deal of social influence, and knew intimately many persons of wealth and culture, who would possibly value his opinion upon a painter's merits at a high figure.

Mr. Luxmore, in short, was a man of the world, and weighed and measured his friendships accordingly.

Personally he might have been taken for a stockbroker of Hebraic origin, and would probably have been rather flattered than otherwise at the comparison. With such men art is a trade, not an inspiration, and they aim at looking like business men rather than Bohemians.

On the occasion of one of his frequent visits to Mr. Luxmore's studio Lord Cranbery came across an unusual specimen of humanity, and one which greatly amused and interested him. This was an American whom the artist had known during his Parisian days, and to whom he was indebted for several important patrons in the States — before his new departure in art, that is to say.

At the moment of Lord Cranbery's entrance this gentleman had turned his back upon Luxmore's latest canvas, and, with his chair tilted back and his long lean legs stretching in an upward direction, the feet reposing on the mantelshelf—in perilous proximity to an exquisite little French statuette of a dancing nymph in gray plaster—looked comfortably uncomfortable. Luxmore was busily engaged in painting, but now and again he cast uneasy glances in the direction of the American, to assure himself of the safety of his nymph.

The studio of the successful artist was—like his pictures—upon a very large scale. Luxmore had too keen a perception of the artistic fitness of things to place his magnificent Titans in a place that might serve to display the minute and delicate creations of a Meissonier or a Tadema.

Rents were high, and good studios rare, in that quarter of Kensington; but Luxmore knew that it would be a fatal mistake in him to study economy in that respect, and therefore installed himself in one of the biggest and handsomest rooms attainable.

Also, he knew exactly how, by the skilful management of accessories, to enhance the effectiveness of his designs. Nothing that taste and money could suggest was wanting to make the beauty and grandeur of his works more apparent. The decorations were in exquisite taste, and of broad and simple hues; the draperies and curtains fell in severe and massive folds. Here and there the severity of the general effect was skilfully broken by the introduction of some subtle touch of colour in a jar or bowl of Oriental china, or the light glanced upon some quaint piece of armour or trophy of savage weapons.

The studio was, in fact, a carefully arranged and thought out sale-room. Yet Zachary Luxmore was a humbug. He worked hard, and loved his profession also. One deep feeling, however, was pre-eminent above his love of art. This was his care for a certain little man called Zachary Luxmore, and that little man's success in life.

Mr. Luxmore was essentially modern. He had made a study of success, and won it.

As he laid down his palette and brushes, and came forward to greet Lord Cranbery, he was a representative type of our popular man — quick, eager, volatile, self-assured, self-asserting. He introduced the lounging gentleman as Mr. Tidd of New York. Mr. Tidd acknowledged the introduction by withdrawing the cigarette from his mouth for an instant, and bowing as gravely and majestically as his position—which he made no attempt to alter—would allow.

Then he carefully scanned from head to

foot, with a pair of large, mournful brown eyes, the young nobleman. Cranbery found this scrutiny decidedly embarrassing. Mr. Tidd—or Marc Aurelius Tidd, as he preferred to hear himself called—was a man whose age it would have been difficult to surmise, but who was as yet probably somewhere in his thirties.

In figure he was spare and loosely-jointed, with an elongated, thin, and yet not unpleasing face, whose most striking characteristic was its expression of resigned sadness. Eyelids, nose, mouth, and moustache alike appeared to droop under some indefinite touch of sorrow, and the eyes never showed a spark of gaiety or of humour, even whilst their owner might be giving utterance to the quaintest speeches, telling the most humorous stories, or indulging in the wildest flights of imagination. His tones were habitually quiet and slow, and with very little of the nasal twang about them. But he was nevertheless unmistakably

Transatlantic. His idioms were more pronounced than his accent.

'Seen the St. Dorothea?' he asked Lord Cranbery, with a backward gesture of the head in the direction of Luxmore's colossal canvas. 'Good-looking young woman, don't you think? Way ahead of all those musty old saints in the Louvre or the Vatican. Tell Luxmore he might as well have called her Dolly, though. Not much of the saint about her, to my way of thinking.'

'Come, come, Tidd, I can't allow you to depreciate my picture,' protested the artist, threatening the speaker with his mahl-stick. The latter waved him aside with careless disdain.

'Say, now, *does* it depreciate a picture to state that it's like flesh and blood rather than the stuff that dreams are made of? Besides, it doesn't matter. You told me once that Lord Cranbery wasn't a buyer.'

Lord Cranbery and Luxmore both laughed outright at Mr. Tidd's blunt frankness.

The conversation soon drifted away from the pictures, fond as Mr. Luxmore usually was of expatiating upon the merits of his work. Lord Cranbery grew intensely interested and amused with his new acquaintance.

It was marvellous, the variety of experiences that Mr. Tidd had encountered during the course of his life. He had evidently been a great traveller, had hunted buffaloes and grizzlies in the Far West, been through the Dark Continent after ivory and lions, gone in heavily for pig-sticking and tiger-hunting in India. He was a devotee of perpetual motion.

And yet the first impression he conveyed to strangers was one of an entirely opposite character. He appeared as the most indolent and lackadaisical of mortals, too lazy even to grow excited over the recital of his own adventures. To be sure, this impression never lasted long. When it passed away it left behind a conviction of intense restlessness and a dominating vitality.

Even when Mr. Marc A. Tidd was sleepily drawling out one of his wild, improbable, laughable stories, he made people feel the presence of a brain intensely and uncomfortably alive. The peculiarity of the thing was that the personal magnetism of the man was so potent that this restlessness of his proved excessively contagious. A spirit of adventure suddenly seized upon the quietest and most home-loving people if he long played the first part in any society.

Lord Cranbery wondered what could have brought such a man to London.

'Cities will have little attraction for you,' he remarked curiously. 'You will want to be off to the wilds again after a week or two of London life, eh?'

Mr. Tidd nodded.

'I don't cotton to them much, I confess,' he said, 'but I have a reason for staying in town at present. Besides, there is my sister. She told me to bring her to Europe, and I obeyed. She's a good girl, is Celia, and stuck to the old folks as long as they lived. I didn't! Sometimes sorry for it now. Selfish, like the rest of men, I reckon. Thought they'd live for ever. They didn't.'

He stopped to flick the ash from his cigarette, and then proceeded:

'Celia says she wants to see the world. I tell her it's all pretty much the same as New York, but she declines to take my word for it, and wants to see for herself. Tolerably good-looking girl, and clever, too. Fancies she would like to marry into the aristocracy. I advise her to be content with a less expensive ambition, but she doesn't take advice generally. Wanted some gowns in Paris. I bought her the gowns—six boxes full; had to pay no end for excess luggage—and now——' Here he hesitated.

'Now you are going to indulge her other fancy!' exclaimed the artist, with a queer and unmirthful laugh. 'By Jove! how I wish I had been born an aristocrat instead of a poor dauber! I would lay my title at her feet without one moment's hesitation! Miss Tidd is an exceedingly charming girl, I can assure you, Lord Cranbery, although our friend's description would not lead you to suppose so.'

'Yes; she's a tolerably good-looking girl,' reiterated Mr. Tidd slowly; 'but I'm not going to buy her a husband, and that's a fact. I think she'll manage to please herself in that way if she chooses. I don't lay much store on the aristocracy myself—no offence to you, Lord Cranbery —but if Celia sets her heart upon any member of the British upper circles she'll manage it somehow. That's Celia!'

Lord Cranbery did not approve of the way in which the American spoke of his sister's ambitions. There appeared to the English gentleman some lack of delicacy in this blunt avowal of the absent Celia's wishes, especially as the remarks were addressed to him. It is true that girls are bought and sold every day in the Babylonian slave-mart, and, indeed, that men do not scorn to sell their own good looks and social standing to the highest bidder of the opposite sex. But humbug is a great convenience, and even a social necessity. Some superficial glamour is generally thrown over these transactions. Their baseness is not the subject of such candid talk.

Lord Cranbery took his leave presently, asking permission as he did so to come again upon an early day, and to bring with him his friend, the Marquis of Carabas, to view the picture Luxmore was engaged upon, which was to be sent abroad shortly, as being a commission from a Russian prince.

As he spoke, the American started slightly, seemed as though he would have spoken, then, catching Luxmore's eye, relapsed into a reverie from which the artist's sharp tongue could scarcely rouse him.

The latter began ironically bewailing the well-known fact that the visitor who had just departed was engaged to his cousin, the Lady Nora Challoner, daughter of the Duke of Dundridge, because had this not been the case he might possibly have suited Miss Tidd in the capacity of husband. He was clever, intellectual, and moral also. To be sure, he was not very rich, but then Miss Celia's fortune would have been all the more welcome.

Beneath all this current of raillery a tinge of bitterness could be detected. A disinterested observer could not have failed to surmise that some personal feeling animated the artist, and that for some reason not immediately apparent he resented the lady's avowed ambition. But the American did not choose to notice this.

'Well, yes. Think he might have done for Celia? Seems harmless enough. Looks bilious, though. Might pass for a New Yorker in that respect,' drawled Mr. Tidd unconcernedly.

Then all at once he seemed to become awake.

'Say, now, Luxmore, who was it he asked leave to bring here along with him? Not sure I caught the name correctly.'

'The Marquis of Carabas. The Marquis is one of our most promising young politicians—one who would have made his mark in the House of Commons had he not been fortunate enough to become heir to a marquisate. One of Cran's cousins—Lady Ermyntrude—is to be married to the Marquis at the close of the season. It is a marriage that satisfies even the Duchess of Dundridge's ambition, and it takes a good deal to do that, I can assure you. You appear familiar with the name. Do you know the Marquis?'

'Well—yes; I *am* tolerably familiar with the name.'

'And the man?' asked Luxmore eagerly, for with him curiosity was a ruling passion.

Mr. Marc A. Tidd looked at him in a quiet and reflective manner before answering, and a significant look dawned in his dark, melancholy eyes.

'You think you scent a mystery or a scandal, my friend,' he said coolly, yawning. Then, rising and lifting his long lean arms above his head in order to free them from the effects of their constrained immovableness: 'Sorry that I can't oblige you with a pretty little bit of something for the club. Yes, I'm tolerably familiar with the name of the Marquis of Carabas. Our journals keep us up in all the doings of your peerage. But the man—the man I know nothing of, that's a fact.'

And with a brief adieu Mr. Tidd lounged out of the studio to avoid further questioning.

While he lighted his cigar in the hall he nodded his head emphatically once or twice. 'Well, yes,' he muttered, as though some doubt were solved, 'if things are as I expect, I shall have to disturb the equanimity of that noble Marquis, although

I don't bear him any malice, seeing that I don't know him even by sight. All the same, I've come to England to find him, and I guess I'll have to make him pretty uncomfortable before I say adieu. But there's no need to spoil matters by precipitation, and Friend Luxmore chatters like a magpie and a blue jay rolled into one. Things get into the society papers quickly enough without my assistance, I surmise.'

END OF VOL. I.

BILLING AND SONS, PRINTERS, GUILDFORD.

www.ingramcontent.com/pod-product-compliance
Lightning Source LLC
Chambersburg PA
CBHW032119230426
43672CB00009B/1791